CW01189332

• HALSGROVE DISCOVER SERIES ➤

THE PEDDARS WAY AND NORFOLK COAST PATH

**STEPHEN BROWNING
AND DANIEL TINK**

HALSGROVE

First published in Great Britain in 2013

Copyright © Stephen Browning and Daniel Tink 2013

All rights reserved. No part of this publication may be reproduced, stored in a retrieval system, or transmitted in any form or by any means without the prior permission of the copyright holder

British Library Cataloguing-in-Publication Data
A CIP record for this title is available from the British Library

ISBN 978 0 85704 221 7

HALSGROVE
Halsgrove House,
Ryelands Business Park,
Bagley Road, Wellington, Somerset TA21 9PZ
Tel: 01823 653777   Fax: 01823 216796
email: sales@halsgrove.com

Part of the Halsgrove group of companies
Information on all Halsgrove titles is available at:
www.halsgrove.com

Printed in China by Everbest Printing Co Ltd

Dedications

Daniel: For my Mum, Leanne and Dad, Barry who loves the North Norfolk Coast.

Stephen: For my Dad, always in my heart.

CONTENTS

	Introduction	5
	The walk ahead – a (very) short history lesson	6
Chapter 1	**Knettishall Heath to Little Cressingham**	8
Chapter 2	**Little Cressingham to Castle Acre**	28
Chapter 3	**Castle Acre to Sedgeford**	40
Chapter 4	**Sedgeford to Holme and Hunstanton**	52
Chapter 5	**Hunstanton to Thornham**	70
Chapter 6	**Thornham to Burnham Deepdale**	74
Chapter 7	**Burnham Deepdale to Holkham**	78
Chapter 8	**Holkham to Stiffkey**	88
Chapter 9	**Stiffkey to Cley**	94
Chapter 10	**Cley to Weybourne**	108
Chapter 11	**Weybourne to Cromer**	114
Chapter 12	**Practical things**	139
Appendix 1	*A guide to some of the place names encountered along the Peddars Way and Norfolk Coast Path*	143
Appendix 2	*Norfolk Songline verses*	144
Appendix 3	*Norfolk language: a few unfamiliar words you may hear on the trail*	144

The place I love most, by Daniel Tink

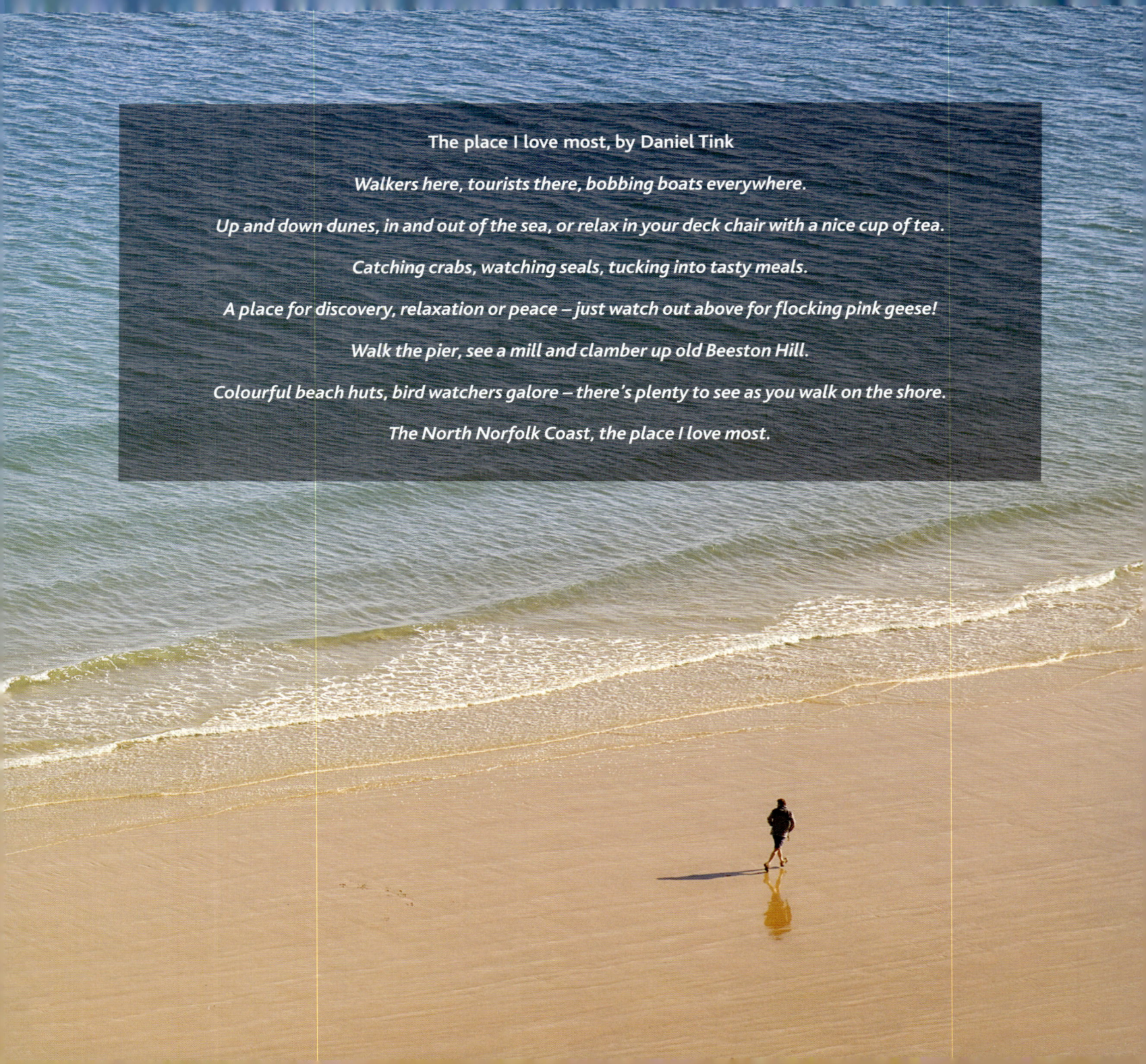

Walkers here, tourists there, bobbing boats everywhere.

Up and down dunes, in and out of the sea, or relax in your deck chair with a nice cup of tea.

Catching crabs, watching seals, tucking into tasty meals.

A place for discovery, relaxation or peace – just watch out above for flocking pink geese!

Walk the pier, see a mill and clamber up old Beeston Hill.

Colourful beach huts, bird watchers galore – there's plenty to see as you walk on the shore.

The North Norfolk Coast, the place I love most.

INTRODUCTION

We very much hope you will enjoy this book. It has been a complete joy to research and put together.

Whilst it contains what we hope are many and varied ideas for things to do on the walk itself, we have also been aware of the need to produce a book that is useful and entertaining both before the walk starts and, when you return home, as a reminder of the glorious trip.

Many walkers may want to tackle the trail taking one section after the other without any detours. However, we discovered so many wonderful sites and paths near, but not actually, *on* the path that we have included our pick of these. They run through the text in special 'boxes' entitled 'JUST OFF THE PATH'. We are told that a super-fit walker can finish both sections of the trail – the Peddars Way and Norfolk Coast Path – in little over three days. Well, I am afraid it took us considerably longer and we thoroughly enjoyed every moment! It is one of the trail's most fantastic features that it is suited to pretty much all ages and abilities, being mostly flat, at least in the 46 miles up to the coast, and you can go at whatever pace you like.

We have tried, along with information on pathways, flora and fauna and so on, to give interesting historical and literary references that will hopefully add to the enjoyment of the walk. There is too, for many, an almost overwhelming spiritual aspect to the journey and we have tried to capture this in words and images. We have not, though, included up-to-date and specific information on hotels, hostels, bus times, prices of goods etc as these are constantly changing and by far the best ways to become updated about these are either via websites – just start by typing 'Peddars Way and Norfolk Coast Path' into your search engine – or by contacting the many and quite excellent tourist information centres that abound in Norfolk.

Thank you. May we wish you a very entertaining read and a memorable walk!

Stephen and Daniel
www.facebook.com/stevebrowningbooks
www.scenicnorfolk.co.uk

Norfolk 2013

THE WALK AHEAD
a (very) short history lesson

'A journey of a thousand miles begins with a single step.'
Lao-tzu, *The Way of Lao-tzu.*
Chinese philosopher (604 BC - 531 BC).

The Peddars Way and the Norfolk Coast Path are two contrasting trails that link at Holme and Hunstanton totalling around 96 miles. The first is basically flat, although with some fascinating and unusual flora and fauna, making it suitable for a very wide range of ages and abilities. The Norfolk Coast Path is very different – spectacular and invigorating, where it is sometimes possible to imagine you are walking on the edge of the world.

The origins of the Peddars Way are by no means clear. Some say it started its life due to the rebellious nature of folk in this part of the world. In AD 60-61 Boudicca had revolted openly against the Roman conquerors and had come within a whisker of throwing them out of the country altogether. Was Peddars Way constructed to make it easy to move legions around the area in order to inflict retribution on the East Angles for their literally bare-faced cheek in defying the might of Rome? Certainly, some parts exhibit obvious Roman engineering feats and we know that the Emperor Nero was so alarmed at the scale of revengeful atrocities that he sacked the governor of the region and despatched an envoy to report back on what was going on.

This is possible, but part of the magic of this first part of the walk – to Holme and Hunstanton – is that we don't know for sure. Does the strangely peculiar straight path of the route suggest that whoever built it wanted to get to the coast in a hurry? Why? Who would have wanted to take the fast route to Holme? (Sorry, present-day Holme, no offence: we highlight your glories later on.)

THE WALK AHEAD

One theory is that the Peddars Way formed part of a much longer path, probably Roman in origin, that connected Lyme Regis to the North Norfolk coast at Hunstanton via Swindon, Reading, Luton and Cambridge. Maybe the invaders would then take a boat across the Wash and continue their way to their northern territories. The only reason they would have done this rather than simply heading due north from the south coast would surely have been because the land structure presented hard, easy ridges in the main. This would in turn have enabled rapid travel for both troops and traders of various sorts.

Some historians argue that the route extended further – to Southampton and Cornwall, which raises a whole host of questions as to its purpose and construction.

It is possible, also, that the route pre-dates the Romans. We know that 500 million years ago Norfolk was contained entirely within what is called the Avalonian Block which, simply put, means that it was joined to present day Europe. It is pure speculation, but it is fascinating to think that maybe the Peddars Way was a main route to important trading bases on the Continent.

Setting off

So, as you reach the car park at Blackwater Carr amidst, in spring, lovely wild flowers and hopping pheasants, you cannot but wonder. And the puzzle will continue. There are clues everywhere – flints, rare animals not naturally indigenous to this part of the world, natural flora as well as sometimes ham-fisted modern attempts at nature subjugation, deserted villages, the Army, ghosts of people who have loved and lost their right to be here – and in this first 'half' of the walk you will form your own impressions. When you reach the coast there is a sea change, both literally and metaphorically, in the nature of the trail that is both exhilarating and sudden.

The sign at Blackwater Carr simply says 'Holme 46 miles'.

Anmer is a small village connected to the Royal Estate at Sandringham by a straight road known as 'The Avenue'. The village sign features a Roman soldier on one side and a boy scout on the other. The Latin inscription says 'Be Prepared'.

Little Cressingham

Peddars Way

Thompson

East Wretham

A11

River Thet

Knettishall Heath

Chapter 1
KNETTISHALL HEATH TO LITTLE CRESSINGHAM

Distance: about 14.5 miles

'Often times within the circle of your sight there is neither house nor man visible. A grey church tower, a windmill, or the dark-brown sail of a wherry in the distance breaks the sense of utter loneliness, but the scene is wild enough to enchain the imagination of many.'

George Chistopher Davis (1884).

Section shapshot: This is mostly gentle walking territory, suitable for all ages. It is rich in wildlife and you will find the first two Songline sculptures (more below) in this stretch. There are, however, a few very busy roads to cross. Best to take a drink and sun cream as it can become very hot. Your mobile phone probably will not work on much of the route.

The land is flat and easy on the whole in this first section. Let us begin!

Right: *There is much man-made activity in this area, such as this lake just off the path. The object is to promote and preserve the natural local species.*

Below and bottom right:
A few minutes into the walk will bring you to the crossing of the Little Ouse River at Blackwater. Hereabouts, glistening in the morning dew, you may spot gigantic cobwebs. You are also quite likely to spot an adder but they are usually quite uninterested in human beings unless provoked.

Knettishall Heath. This country park is adjacent to our starting point and is the hub of local long distance paths – Peddars Way; Icknield Way – probably dating back to at least 4000 BC and taking you 120 miles into Buckinghamshire; and Angles Way which finishes almost 80 miles away in Great Yarmouth. You may see some semi-wild Exmoor ponies, descended from Britain's indigenous wild species dating back over 100,000 years. The land has woodland vistas, riverside walks, heath and meadows with patches of both acid and chalky soils.

Your path will pass alongside some deep tilled soil and spectacular, mighty trees. The jay has historically been responsible for many of the latter – it has been estimated that each will 'hide' up to 5000 acorns each spring and summer to theoretically retrieve for food in winter.

On a beautiful spring morning, the path in this section is a paradise for everyone – from well-equipped couples and single trekkers to mums, children and the family pet.

This is a beautiful and easy start to the path with streams, wild flowers, wooden bridges and paths beside dark brown, tilled fields. It is a favourite stroll for families prior to Sunday lunch and you may well see many more people on this initial stretch than you will anywhere else on the trail – at least until you get to Holme. We also highlight some sites of great interest just off the path.

**JUST OFF THE PATH
(2 miles north of
Brandon, off B1106)
WEETING CASTLE.**
This is all that remains of a manor house with a moat around it for protection. It was built by Hugh de Plais in the twelfth century and probably abandoned by the 1500s. The southern section had a three storey lookout tower. It is cared for now by English Heritage and can be visited all year round.

A *more lightly wooded section.*

**JUST OFF THE PATH
(4 miles north east of Brandon: a mile north of Grimes Graves)
LYNFORD**

This is a site of international scientific importance. Excavations have revealed new details of life from maybe 50,000 years ago including nine woolly mammoths, an extremely rare woolly rhino and a bear. Fossils of over 100 species of insects and dozens of flint hand axes have also been found – the flints would of course have come from nearby Grimes Graves.

**JUST OFF THE PATH
(2 miles west of Thetford, off B1107) THETFORD WARREN LODGE**

Most people are surprised to learn that rabbits are not indigenous to the UK but were introduced by the Normans about a thousand years ago. At first they did not acclimatise well and so were protected and cared for by specially trained men called 'warreners'. Thetford Warren Lodge would have been the home of the warrener to the Prior of Thetford. Here we see a fortified building designed for lookout and defence against gangs of poachers: note the windows on the first storey which would have been utilised for pouring noxious liquids, rocks etc onto the heads of those below.

The rabbit industry grew to be an important part of the local economy until comparatively recently. As late as 1900 two hundred thousand rabbits were bred firstly for their meat, but then also for their skins. Many local people gained home employment in part of this process – first the hair would be removed to make 'rabbit wool' and this, when combined with other materials to give it additional strength, made extremely high grade felt. Also, rabbit-skin gloves were considered the hight of fashion in London. Any poor grade skin or bits and pieces left over were used to make glue.

There is reported to be a ghost of a large white rabbit with foaming eyes which hops around after sunset, any sighting of which heralds disaster.

Some flowers to be seen on the path: hawthorn blossom; celandine; the predatory purple loosestrife.

> **JUST OFF THE PATH**
> **(west side of Thetford by railway station) THETFORD PRIORY**
>
> This, the Cluniac Priory of Our Lady of Thetford, was once one of the most important religious sites in England. It was founded by Roger Bigod, one of William the Conqueror's trusted followers, in 1107. He died the following week, his life's work accomplished. There was reputed to have subsequently been a miraculous appearance of the Virgin Mary and pilgrims flocked to the site. Repair work has been carried out in recent years, in part funded by money from the European Union.
>
> A short distance away is the church of the Holy Sepulchre, all that remains of a fourteenth century priory.
>
> Thetford Castle mound, or motte, is said to have been created by the devil scraping his boot as it was muddy after he had made the Fen-dyke at Weeting. It is the second largest such man-made motte in England. A small pond can be found in a hollow north east of the northern rampart. If you walk around this seven times at midnight, so legend has it, you will meet St Nick himself.

Throughout this part of the walk you will be nipping in and out of Thetford Forest. This is the largest man-made forest in England – about 200 square kilometres, about a quarter of which is the Stanford Battle Area – a fascinating part about which we talk a little later.

'Every land and every sea
Have I crossed, but much the worst
Is the land of Norfolk cursed.
That the land is poor and bad
I the clearest proof have had.
If you plant the choicest wheat
Tares and darnel you will meet.
Satan on the road to Hell
Ruined Norfolk as he fell '.

Traditional verse about the 'Brecks', reputedly written by a frustrated monk about a thousand years ago.

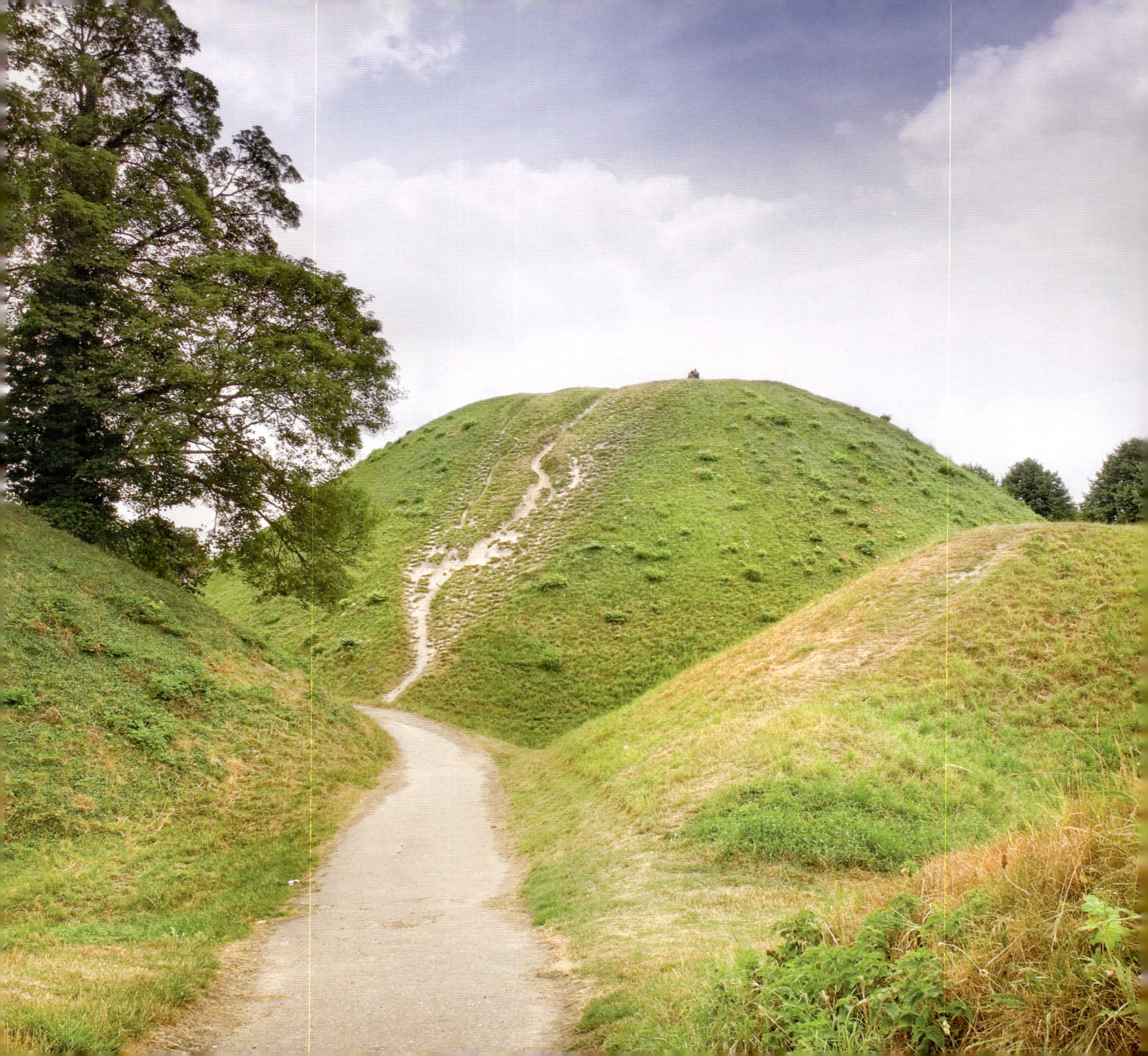

It is reported in the Domesday Book that this area was home to herds of wild horses. However, the soil became less and less suitable to provide sustenance for these gracious creatures. Just a hundred years ago, the area was only a sandy desert. Rabbits, as we say above, were bred here both for their meat and fur. The black rabbit was particularly prized as it provided exotic and supersoft fur for 'my lady's dress'. But apart from this, the land had precious little commercial potential. The whole area was christened 'The Brecks' – broken land – by writer WG Clarke in 1894. This wonderful writer was, however, very much in love with the local landscape which varies tremendously when spring is over. He gives a poetic account of the local colour each summer (Norfolk and Suffolk, A. and C. Black 1921):

'The gorgeousness of the varying blooms is wonderful. A not infrequent sight is a big field of orange kidney vetch, with splashes of bluish purple viper's bugloss and ruddy-purple nodding thistle, the delicate green of the Canadian fleabane, the shimmer of silky hair grass, and a mat of purple, pink and white basil thyme, with the occasional scarlet of a poppy. Here there is no stint of colour or perfume, both running over with a prodigality not often noticed except on the 'breck' sands. One is rarely away from the scent of the pine woods, the pungent odour of the bracken, the smell of lady's bedstraw or of the many acres of blossoming kidney vetch.'

> **'Long and delightful was the dream,**
> **A waking dream that Fancy yields,**
> **Till with regret I left the stream**
> **And plung'd across the barren fields'.**
> From *In Breckland Wilds* by R. Rainbird Clarke 1974.

Following the First World War, the government initiated a massive tree planting scheme (Scots and Corsican pine being found particularly suitable). The trees, once mature, are thinned, new ones being planted from local seedlings. Thus there is continual renewal. The wood is used in the construction industry and for paper and pulp.

Animals, birds, butterflies and fungi

Quiet and stark in parts, Thetford Forest is not – summer apart – the kind of place to throw its charms at you. And yet, for children and nature lovers, there is so much to see with an abundance of clues all around as you walk. A good pair of binoculars will really help.

A magical sight is to look up to quite unexpectedly see a deer staring straight at you from a short distance away. Look away for a split second and it is gone. The huge red, roe and muntjac deer live here.

Opposite: *The mound – motte – of Thetford Castle was reputedly made by the Devil as he scraped off his boot having just created the Fen-dyke at Weeting.*

Grey and, much less common, red squirrels can also be seen. If you come across any stripped pine cones, it is a sign that the red squirrel is close by as its favourite food is pine seeds.

The planting of the forest has resulted in a change in the species of birds to be seen. The woodlark and stone curlew are now very rare. However woodland jays and sparrowhawks thrive as does the very rare crossbill. You may not see a crossbill as they like to stay very high up in the trees but again, if you come across some pine cones from which the seeds have been almost surgically extracted leaving the cone more or less intact – they have amazing curved beaks – it is a sign that there may be a crossbill or two way above where you are standing.

Golden pheasants are also bred here. These magnificent and colourful birds can be very aggressive if you venture near their breeding spots. They can block the path or chase you and fearlessly attack your walking boots if they have a mind so it is a good idea to keep a sharp eye. They also do not appreciate being harassed by dogs and can hold their own in a scrap!

Other varieties of birds in various parts of the forest and The Brecks in general include redstart, nightingale, woodcock, siskin, nightjar, goshawk, hawfinch corn bunting, ringed plover, lapwing, tree sparrow, grey partidge, kingfisher, snipe and golden oriole. Many teachers will bring groups of students here to thrillingly identify these species which the

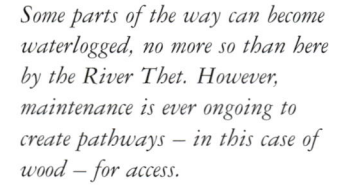

Some parts of the way can become waterlogged, no more so than here by the River Thet. However, maintenance is ever ongoing to create pathways – in this case of wood – for access.

KNETTISHALL HEATH TO LITTLE CRESSINGHAM

students have previously studied only in class.

Some folk like to come here armed with a fungi-indentification book – the shaggy ink cap, sulphur tuf, and the commonly named conifer heartrot which attacks the trees, are some of many varieties which thrive on the decaying plants in the forest. Needless to say, some are poisonous and should not be touched without expert advice.

A find of deer antlers in Grimes Graves, probably late nineteenth century. (lantern slide, reproduced with permission, Picture Norfolk Library).

Grimes Graves. Grimes Graves is a Neolithic flint mining complex situated 7 miles north west of Thetford. It was first mentioned in Camden's *Britannia* in 1695 where the pock-marked landscape was seen as evidence of deep shafts – there are at least 433 – which it is suggested denoted a vast underground encampment capable of hiding an entire army. Or could it have been an Iceni underground city? Some people think so.

Although controversy still exists on some aspects of the site, especially exactly *when* it operated, it is now agreed that it was a flint mining site. Most experts think that it was worked between 3000 BC and about 1900 BC. Shafts were dug in order to reach the third seam of flint, named 'floorstone' as this was superior to the seams nearer to the surface. Then shafts were dug horizontally and the flint excavated. It was used for flint axes, for building and, much later, as strikers for muskets.

Deer antlers were used as picks and as these tended to not last too long, it is certain that a deer farm must have also operated here. There is also evidence of human bones being used which may in turn be an indication of cannibalism and a corresponding lack of respect for the bodies of the dead.

Why Grimes Graves? 'Grim' was a euphemism for the God 'Woden' and 'Graves' simply means 'Quarries'. Hence 'Woden's' – or 'the Masked One's' quarries'. Some have it that the site has an altogether more sinister aspect and that the real name is 'the Devil's Graves'.

The flints would be taken to various villages in the region to be worked. Initially, they would have been fashioned into axes or other implements. It is interesting that this was one of the longest surviving industries in Britain, thriving right up to the 1930s.

In the age of muskets, expert 'knappers' would take the flints and, by striking the flint at exactly the right spot, produce flakes which were used as gunflints. Flints would be worked primarily at nearby Brandon.

Interesting to note in the present day world where almost absolutely every product has a natty catchphrase, Brandon flints had one of the first: *'Brandon flint – more certain in its fire and lasting longer than any other'*. Brandon flint knappers were seen as supreme in their craft.

The knapper would sit, protected by a strong apron and produce as many as several hundred gunflints an hour working with the flint on his lap. The peak of the industry was at the time of the Napoleonic Wars when Brandon supplied over 300,000 gunflints a month to Wellington's men.

Other uses of flint were in building and, for prestigious work – Norwich has some fine examples – a large flint would be 'knapped' to produce a square. The Guildhall, centre of governance for the city since the fifteenth century, is a supreme example of using squared, knapped flints to beautiful effect. Some churches, especially in the Coslany area of the city, have beautiful squared knapped walls, although expense dictated that often only those parts of the building 'on show', ie facing the roadway, were built in this way.

Many churches in the Norfolk countryside have interesting flint work, Mildenhall, Lyndford, Elveden, and St Peter's church, Thetford among them. Thetford Warren Lodge, which we feature, is one of a number of defensive structures built utilising flint.

There is some controversy as to other uses for the pits at Grimes Graves. Artefacts, including some of a sexual nature, which were uncovered in 1939, may point to ritualistic and religious uses, although it is possible that these objects were fakes, deliberately planted by persons unknown who wanted to mislead and have some fun. No doubt more surprises await us and future generations.

Grimes Graves is in the care of English Heritage and is open to the public. You can descend into a 12 ft pit. Opening times can be found on the English Heritage website.

Flint knapping at Brandon, late nineteenth century (reproduced with permission, Picture Norfolk Library).

This is pingo country. Pingos date back over 20,000 years to the last ice age. 'Pingo' comes from an Inuit word meaning ' small hill of ice'. Ice below the surface froze and this pushed the soil upwards. During the summer, as temperatures increased, the surface soil would become sludge and fall back to the edges of the small crater. Finally, the ice would melt leaving pingos as we see them today.

Circular Pingo Trail

You can gain access to an 8 mile round pingo trail from several points in this vicinity. The trail goes through Stow Bedon common, Stow, Breckles Heath, Hockham Heath, Peddars Way, past Stanford Training Area and Thompson Water. This latter is a lake of about 40 acres which was artificially created in 1845 and is an important wintering site for wildfowl. More details www.countrysideaccess.norfolk.gov.uk

THE PEDDARS WAY AND NORFOLK COAST PATH

The area has many species of dragon and damsel flies and, in winter, wildfowl. Also, alas, it is an ideal breeding ground for mosquitos, so an insect repellent is highly recommended.

The Dreaming and a Norfolk Songline

Throughout the Peddars Way, you will be aware of 'The Dreaming' . We now have to nip to Australia for a moment. For many indigenous Australians ' The Dreaming' refers to the time when the world was created. Before animals and plants came into being in a physical sense, their souls existed and everything a living person does leaves a mark on the earth. Thus we all have a duty to be careful as to how we treat our environment which was created, quite literally, by archetypal beings. Everything – physical, spiritual or in essence is part of a vast song which has no beginning and no end.

A Norfolk Songline derives from these beliefs and is part of an arts project that runs along the whole of the Peddars Way. You will be physically reminded of this by five sculptures created by Tom Perkins, on the trail. Other artists have created a spoken and sung CD and book for purchase, as well as a teaching pack for schools.

A dragonfly rests – the area is home to many species of these magnificent creatures.

The Army takes over

Seven miles north of Thetford lies the Stanford Battle Area which is a training facility for the British Army covering about 30,000 acres. Military activity began here during the First World War but it was in 1942 that the government completely evacuated the villages of Buckenham Tofts, Langford, Stanford, Sturston, Tottington and West Tofts. The locals were promised that their gardens would be available for them to harvest and their homes treated with care. Alas, this was not to be as ebullient troops drove tanks straight through both. Residents were also assured of a return to their homes after the war but this has not been the case either. Some churches are still cared for very well by the Army and are available for special occasions and burials, the area thus presenting an eerie and other-wordly vista to the visitor (entry to the area is only available by special request and application must be made to the Ministy of Defence).

A 'Nazi village' was established and important exercises undertaken here in the run-up to D-Day.

In 2009, in perhaps the absolute as regards acclimatisation for troops about to be posted overseas, an 'Afghan village' was established, at a cost reputed to have been £14 million, complete with Afghan nationals, Gurkhas and wounded soldiers. Machines flood the village with smells like fetid vegetables, meat that has gone off and raw sewage.

The Red Lion Inn at West Tofts before the Army takeover (reproduced with permission, Picture Norfolk Library).

Opposite: *A pingo at Thompson.*

Some flowers to be seen on the path: wild foxgloves (digitalis); snowdrops.

A tale of mystery and heartbreak

In the late nineteenth century, the daughter of a carpenter in the area had an illegitimate daughter whom she named Lucilla. Her father was never known, even her birth certificate being blank on this point. Lucilla grew up to be a very colourful character, being of blunt no-nonsense nature and very good with a gun. She farmed here and was reluctant to leave in 1942 but was eventually persuaded to leave upon a promise that she could return when hostilities ended. She also received £800 compensation. However, in 1945 she began a fruitless five year campaign to regain her land, eventually being told by the government that she would never be allowed to return. This broke her heart and, on Remembrance Sunday 1950, she hanged herself. Her faithful dog refused for a long time to let anyone near her body. She was buried in unconsecrated ground on the edge of Tottington church as suicide victims were not allowed to be buried inside church land. In time, however, the boundary of the graveyard was increased and she thus now lies in the confines of the church in which she had worshipped for many years.

Being a protected area, many varieties of wild life in the broadest sense thrive here. The great crested newt, the stone curlew and woodlark have each made a home. 600 registered flowering plants, 28 of which are classified as rare, have been identified, as well as over 30 varieties of butterfly and 400 moths. The water systems support the otter – reintroduced in the 1990s – as well as brown trout, dace, eel and pike.

This section of the walk ends at Little Cressingham. The civil parish contains two ecclesiastical parishes – Little Cressingham and Threxton, the former perhaps deriving in meaning from 'homestead where cress is grown'. As both settlements are mentioned in the Domesday Book, it would seem that the area thrived in early Roman times: a further clue as to their 'heyday' is that many exciting late Iron Age and Roman archaeological finds have been made – particularly coins, pottery and military items. This suggests that a garrison and Roman town existed here until probably about 400 AD.

There is a Bronze Age barrow cemetery at Hopton Farm where, in 1849, there was a spectacular find – a skeleton with a gold breastplate and gold bracelet. Unfortunately for archaeologists, some barrows have been flattened by ploughing but aerial photography has detected the outlines of a great many.

All Saints' church, Threxton, started during Norman times but finished over the next few hundred years, is very pretty. St Andrew's at Little Cressingham is now partly ruined. Both churches were substantially renovated in mid-Victorian times.

A 'must-see' before you walk on is Little Cressingham's combined water and windmill: this has sets of stones operated by both waterwheel and sails and has been restored by the Norfolk Windmill Trust.

Don't chat to everyone!

The Peddars Way and Norfolk Coast Path fulfil different functions for different folk. As we approached the end of this section, the authors saw one chap from some way off – a big guy, laden down with pots and pans and the whole kitchen sink of paraphernalia. He seemed to be singing and very happy. He was walking towards us and, as we came ever nearer, we thought he might be a good 'bet' for a few words. However, he darted into the pines away from us. By complete co-incidence, we unexpectedly came across him a few days later in a different part of the walk. He was sitting alongside a stream and we almost fell over him. 'Oh, Hi! You two,' he said. 'Hope you weren't offended the other day. I come here to walk and be alone! No offence, I hope!'

'Absolutely none taken!' we replied.

East Wretham – here we see the Dog and Partridge pub – is perfect for a stop-off before exploring the Heath, situated six miles north east of Thetford. Once an airfield and later a resettlement camp for Polish fighters, East Wretham Heath now provides ideal conditions for native plants such as viper's bugloss, sheeps' sorrel and forget-me-not. You may also espy adders, the Essex skipper butterfly and rare birds including the woodlark, teal and skylark.

JUST OFF THE PATH
Waylands Wood is just outside of Watton which is at the crossroads of the A1075 Dereham-Thetford Road and the B1108 Brandon-Norwich Road. This is the setting for the 'Babes in the Wood' story. In the mid- sixteenth century, two orphaned children were left in the care of an uncle who handed them over to cut-throats in order to ensure their death and inheritance. However, the men could not go through with the murders and abandoned the children in the woods. Unable to look after themselves, they died and their bodies were covered in leaves by the birds and forest creatures. They were never found but, to this day, haunt the forest.

THE PEDDARS WAY AND NORFOLK COAST PATH

Overlooking the way.

KNETTISHALL HEATH TO LITTLE CRESSINGHAM

Castle Acre

Peddars Way

Great Palgrave

A47

Swaffham

North Pickenham

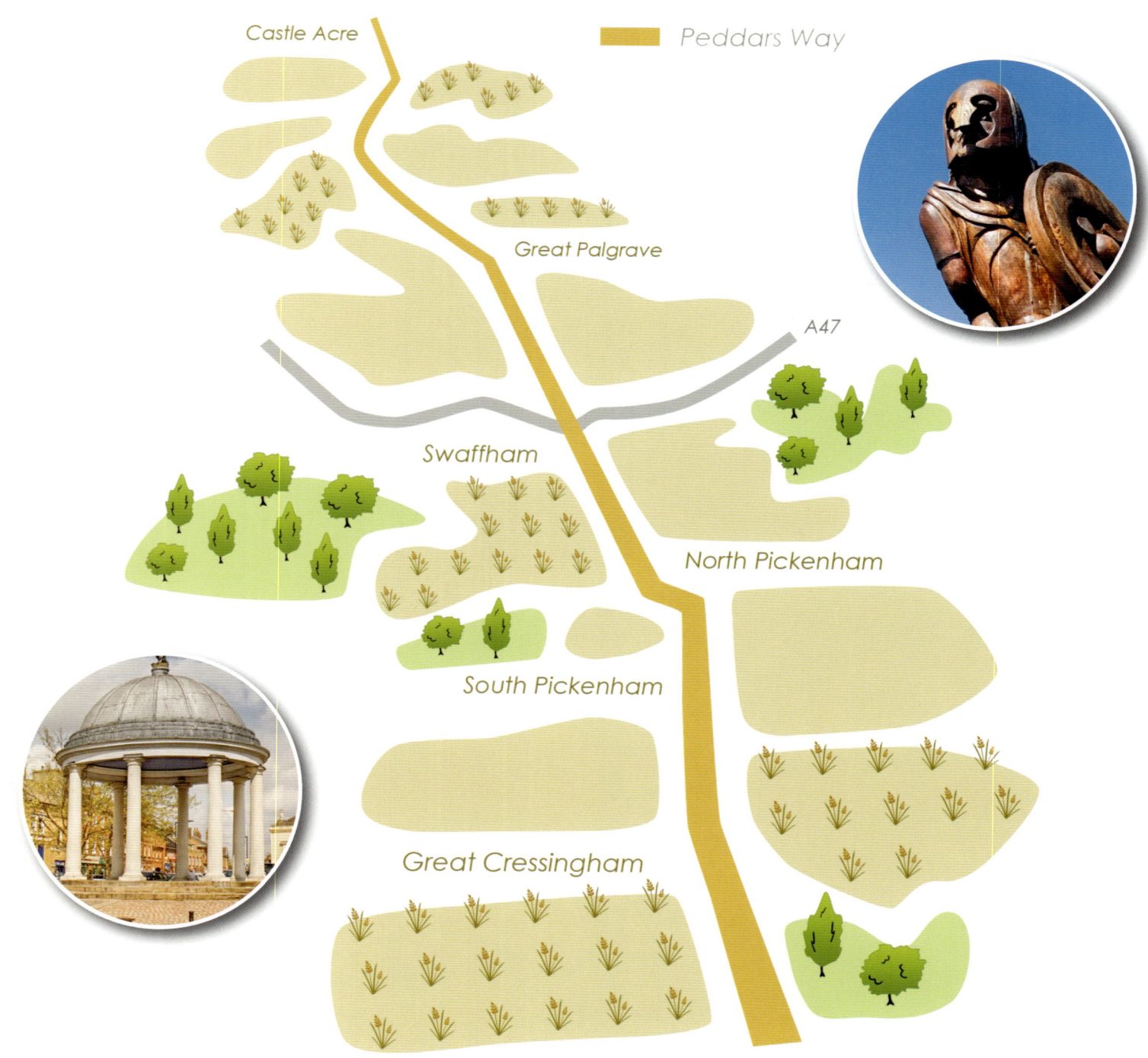

South Pickenham

Great Cressingham

Little Cressingham

Chapter 2
LITTLE CRESSINGHAM TO CASTLE ACRE

Distance: 11.7 miles

'Norfolk would not be Norfolk without a church tower on the horizon or round a corner up a lane. We cannot spare a single Norfolk church. When a church has been pulled down the county seems empty or is like a necklace with a jewel missing.'

Sir John Betjeman.

Little Cressingham is famous for having one of the very first water mills which was also wind assisted when needed. Today, this part of the county is fittingly a world leader in the design, construction and operation of industrial wind turbine systems.

Section snapshot: In this section of the trail, history is never far away. Catherine of Aragon and other pilgrims to Walsingham rested here. Watch out for the third Songline sculpture.
Alternative shorter walk: North Pickenham to Castle Acre: 5.5 miles.

A complete small village

Great Cressingham is situated near the River Wissey – a spread-out settlement which had 279 residents at the time of the 2001 census which is just over half of the number recorded in the mid nineteenth century. At that time it held a famous Horse fair on first Wednesday in August. The original holder of the parish was the Bishop of Thetford.

Great Cressingham sign and the church of St Michael.

It is on the very edge of the Stanford Battle Area, highlighted above.

A school for 140 children was built in 1840 and paid for by the rector. In those days it was very much a complete community: some of the livings of the residents in the mid nineteenth century are recorded as: blacksmith, baker, shoemaker, rector, wheelwright, gent, schoolmaster, cattle dealer, curate, farmer, beerhouse keeper, butcher, shopkeeper, and parish clerk.

The church is dedicated to St Michael in the Benefice of Cockley Cley.

Valuable finds

As in many parts of this area, interesting finds have been made, including Neolthic flints and axeheads. Iron Age and Roman pottery is occasionally uncovered although no further evidence of settlements in these periods exists. Similar fragments suggest that Early and Middle Saxon people lived here. By the time of the Domesday Book Great Cressingham is recorded as a wealthy settlement with fisheries and mills. Aerial pictures suggest a more substantial church than exists today, probably dating from about 1100. The present church, St Michael's, was begun in the thirteenth century.

This part of the walk is largely on metalled surfaces, mostly very pleasant country lanes surrounded by farms. The original Peddars Way path is often lost. Crossing the Great Cressingham road, you will soon see the impressive Pickenham Hall (built 1903).

Zig-zagging down towards the River Wissey and then up, you will emerge on the edge of North Pickenham village. You will see the outline of the church of St Mary, Houghton-on-the-Hill which has recently been renovated. Pickenham is also famous for its airfield. This was the home of the American 492nd Bomber Group who flew 64 missions with B-24 Liberators

The lovely church of All Saints' in South Pickenham. Inside is the extraordinary and exquisite organ of Augustus Pugin, transferred from West Tofts for which it was originally built before the Army took over the region.

There has been a settlement at North Pickenham for at least 1500 years as this carved statue of a Saxon warrior reminds us.

LITTLE CRESSINGHAM TO CASTLE ACRE

in 1944: more than 50 aircraft were lost. Subsequently the RAF took over the site and nuclear missiles were temporarily set up here before being dismantled in 1963.

There are some stiles along the route and the fields are privately owned. However, this was an area frequently travelled by pilgrims on their way to Walsingham. Henry VI passed this way in1447 as did Catherine of Aragon in 1517.

The Thetford-Swaffham railway line is no more but you can still see remnants of it as you approach Dalton's Plantation. Here the Swaefas Way footpath will take you into Swaffham.

Swaffham – Norfolk's favourite town?

Swaffham is named after the Swabian Rhineland immigrants who originally settled here. A Benedictine priory for women was established around the middle of the twelfth century. It is true that women were allowed no education of any commercial value at this time but one lifestyle that was available to them was to serve the Lord. Thus we find – in the rural outposts of Norfolk especially – some thriving priories for ladies.

The Buttercross, Swaffham.

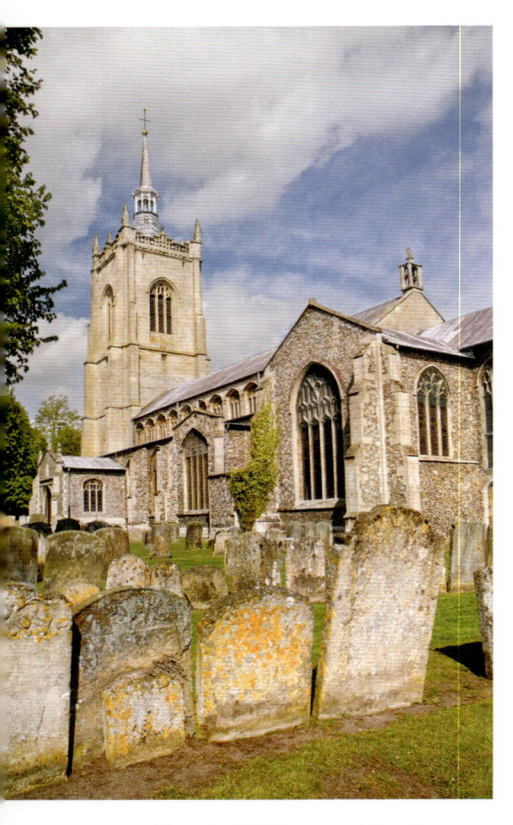

Church of SS Peter and Paul which dominates the skyline at Swaffham.

The town became famous for wool and sheep as times passed and the current Market Cross symbolised this wealth. It was presented to the town by the 3rd Earl of Orford in 1783. The statue on the top is of Ceres, the Roman goddess of harvest.

> **'Here lies the body of Thomas Parr.**
> **What, Old Tom? No.**
> **What, Young Tom? Ah.'**
> Epitaph in Swaffham Church (from East Anglian Epitaphs,
> Raymond Lamont-Brown, Acorn Editions 1981).

On the west side of the market place you will find a plaque commemorating the famous Hammonds Grammar School. A noted art master there in the 1960s was Harry Carter, responsible for many of the wonderful village signs around Norfolk.

His distant cousin was Howard Carter, the famous archaeologist who discovered the tomb of Tutankhamun. The eminent archaeologist entered the tomb in 1922, and was reputed to have consequently died from the curse of the Pharoahs – in reality from cancer – in 1939. He was buried in London and his tomb bears the legend : *'May your spirit live, May you spend millions of years, You who love Thebes, Sitting with your face to the north wind, Your eyes beholding happiness'*.

Harry Carter's most renowned sign is probably that of Swaffham itself. This depicts the Pedlar of Swaffham. Here is the tale, taken from *Norfolk: Exploring the Land of the Wide Skies* by Daniel Tink and Stephen Browning (Halsgrove 2011).

The legend of John Chapman

The story goes that Swaffham church was paid for entirely by a pedlar, John Chapman, who dreamed that if he made his way to London Bridge, something wonderful would be told to him. He made his way to London with great difficulty – this was in the sixteenth Century and he had no money – where he stood on London Bridge for some hours until a man came up to him and asked him what he was doing there. John Chapman told the truth – he was, he said, obeying the instructions in a dream. The other scoffed and said what a foolish thing it was to believe in dreams. ' For if I was as stoop-ud as thee, I would believe a dream I have just had in which I was told that a man, called John Chapman from a town called Swaffham in the county of Norfolk has a tree in his garden under which is a pot of money. Fooey! Thou art a siller owld fule!'

As fast as he could, John Chapman scurried back home to Swaffham and dug under the tree in his garden. Lo!There was a box – but it was empty. On the lid was a Latin inscription which, not understanding, he placed in his front window. Presently some learned scholars came walking by and in voices John Chapman could hear, translated the inscription:

> *'Under me doth lie*
> *Another much richer than I'*

He dug again, and deeper. He discovered a great treasure and, to show his gratitude to God, he paid the entire cost of building the church.

The church itself is magnificent, built largely of Barnack stone which was expensive: whoever paid for it – and I would like to believe every word of the legend – was very wealthy.

A time in the sun: unlikely but true

Many Norfolk villages and town have had their 'moment in the sun', so to speak, but Swaffham's was more spectacular than your average. In the late eighteenth and early nineteenth centuries it was no less than a social centre to rival almost anywhere on the Continent.

Its fine houses and finer roads welcomed the aristocracy to balls, soirées and concerts: aristocratic parents would bring their daughters here 'for the season' and hope thereby to gain a suitable husband.

Lord Orford is reputed to have raced his greyhounds around the countryside known as the Brecks, adjacent to the town and discussed already. Thus he founded the sport. In the eighteenth century, horse racing attracted many visitors but this became overshadowed from 1776 when the Earl of Orford set up a four day event for greyhounds, offering a prize of fifty guineas, a vast amount of money at the time.

A pub in the town is called The Greyhound Inn and it was here that his Lordship founded the first coursing club in 1776.

Visitors are sometimes surprised by the quality of the town's houses but that is because the finest date from this period. Much of the hit TV series *Kingdom*, starring Stephen Fry, was filmed here (The Greyhound Inn becoming The Startled Duck in the series).

A very rare distinction indeed

Another noted citizen was Sir Arthur Knyvet Wilson, one of a select few Royal Navy officers to win the Victoria Cross. He was born in the town in 1842 and died there in 1921, his last job having been to help lead the Navy through the First World War. He is not as famous as the county's premier son, Lord Nelson, being far more self-effacing – and there is not a great deal 'self-effacing' about Admiral Lord Nelson, Duke of Brönte – but, arguably, even more significant in keeping the enemy from the UK's shores.

THE PEDDARS WAY AND NORFOLK COAST PATH

Swaffham's glory is faded now. Even so, just wandering around the town is very nice. If you like cycling, a leaflet is available in the town which will guide you round the Brecks Cycling Discovery Route. Similar trails exist for horse riders.

'Here lieth one, believe it if you can,
Who tho' an attorney was an honest man,
The gates of heaven shall open wide,
But will be shut against all the tribe beside.'

Epitaph at Swaffham
On a Lawyer.

SOME INTERESTING FACTS ABOUT SWAFFHAM

Swaffham was described in 1845 as holding 'a pleasant and highly salubrious situation on the crown of as lofty eminence…'

The air was seen as very healthy, contributing to long life – a Mrs Cross reached the age of 100 in 1816.

In 1797 a cricket match was held between Norfolk and All England, narrowly won by the latter who shared a prize pot of five hundred guineas. Nonetheless, Norfolk became the supreme champions of cricket in England over the next century.

On November nineteenth, 1775, much of the town was destroyed by a disastrous fire. The population then was just over 2000.

Up until the nineteenth century, townsfolk were exempt from serving on juries except in their own parishes. This was one of the privileges of being an 'ancient demesne'.

W.E. Johns, author of the 'Biggles' books, was another famous resident and, upon his death in 1968, had written almost 100 volumes.

Well known modern admirers of the town include Celia Imrie, Baroness Gillian Shephard, Stella Rimmington and Stephen Fry. ' There's something about the place,' writes Stephen Fry, 'a perfect market town, perfectly placed in the heart of Norfolk's perfect Breckland.'

After crossing the A47 you will come to the two deserted medieval villages of Great and Little Palgrave.

Castle Acre

The entrance to Castle Acre is here in lovely waterside country and it is easy to see why the settlement came about in this particular spot.

Castle Acre is also a good place for an overnight stay. In the 2001 census it had a population of about 800.

Do wander around Castle Acre Castle and Priory which lie to the east and west of the village respectively. This is a rarity in that it is a complete Norman settlement – castle, church, village and priory. William de Warrenne built, first, a large stone house but, during the twelfth century the uncertain times dictated immense defensive works which can still be seen today and are very impressive – remains of stone walls and huge ditched earthworks. The north gate survives. You can trace the original street layout inside the gate. William de Warren and his wife, Gundreda – daughter of William the Conqueror, no less – were so impressed with the French monastery at Cluny that they brought members of the order back to England.

Castle Acre has several pretty tea houses/hotels in which to take a break.

Below left: *Follow the track along the ruined walls and out into the countryside…*

Below right: *Castle Acre Priory, interior, probably nineteenth century* (reproduced with permission, Picture Norfolk Library).

We have an idea of how hard life was in the Cluniac Order from a book, published in 1853, by the Revd J.H. Bloom, vicar of Castle Acre and Chaplain in Ordinary to His Royal Highness The Duke of Sussex. This was the day's itinerary for worship:

Mattins	3 a.m.
Prime	6 a.m.
Tierce	9 a.m.
Sext	Noon
Nones	2 p.m.
Vespers	4 p.m.
Compline, or Second Vespers	7 p.m.

Revd Bloom also quotes one Guy de Provins, about monastic life:
> 'When you wish to eat, they make you fast. The night is passed in praying in the church; the day in working; and there is no repose but in the refectory; – and what is to be found there? Rotten eggs, beans with all their pods on, and liquor fit for oxen; for the wine is so poor that one might drink it for a month without intoxication.'

There is a great deal of fascination to see here. Stones tell stories or at least suggest them.

Castle Acre has been farmed for at least two thousand years: we know that, in Saxon times, peas, beans and carrots as well as fruit were grown here.

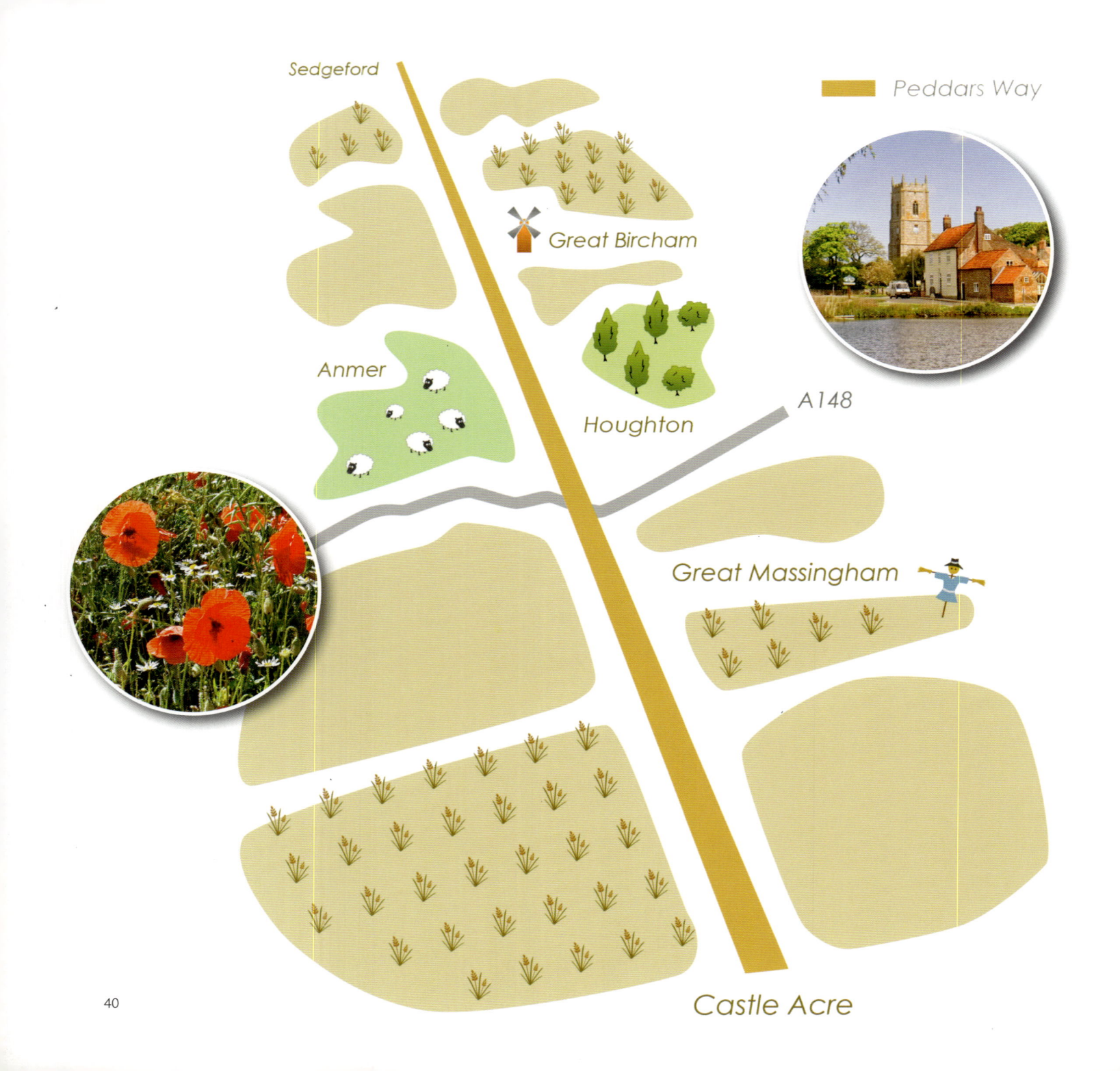

Sedgeford

Peddars Way

Great Bircham

Anmer

Houghton

A148

Great Massingham

Castle Acre

40

Chapter 3
CASTLE ACRE TO SEDGEFORD

Distance: 13.9 miles

'Norfolk is cut off on three sides by the sea and on the fourth by British Rail.'
Local saying.

Section snapshot: This section begins with an almost 3 mile stretch of uphill road. The whole route is very straightforward on mostly hard grassy track or metalled road. Sometimes you will find a specially created track running parallel to the road itself which makes the walk safer and more interesting. Marl pits – used for land improvement on this old heathland at the beginning of the twentieth century – are scattered around. The fourth Songline sculpture is here.

This is the easy way to see some of the trail!

THE PEDDARS WAY AND NORFOLK COAST PATH

Above left to right: *Peddars Way sign north of Castle Acre; Markers on the trail just north of Castle Acre.*

This part of the path is fabulous cycling territory.

You will pass through Shepherd's Bush, one of the highest points on the Norfolk part of the Way at 92 metres and, to the north are the villages of Little Massingham and Great Massingham. Some of the fields here now produce cereals but they are quite 'new' – in the 1930s work began to clear the heath of gorse and bracken, adding lime and manure. A collection of buildings in the middle of nothing else will alert you to the sight of the crossing over the Fakenham-Kings Lynn railway which was closed in 1963.

Great Massingham is a small village famous for its ponds and ducks. Like many other Norfolk villages, the name probably derives from the first important family to settle here in

THE PEDDARS WAY AND NORFOLK COAST PATH

Views of Great Massingham, famous for its ponds and ducks. The church is dedicated to St Mary.

the fifth century – the Maersings. There is great community spirit locally with a regular newsletter and organised rambles on many weekends along the large number of footpaths that surround the village.

Like much of Norfolk, Great Massingham's relative isolation from the rest of England ended in spectacular style 1939-45. Norfolk became the front line of battle. RAF Great Massingham played a significant part in the Second World War, flying Blenheims, Mosquitos and Bostons. Casualties were sometimes heart-breakingly heavy but the sacrifices of these brave men and women will never be forgotten in the local area or farther afield. Many men, especially those from the East – Poles and Czechs – married local girls and stayed on. Many moved to Norwich, the region's capital, and there are some moving memorials to their valour in Norwich Roman Catholic Cathedral. (Interestingly, this wonderful building sits on the highest land in the city and was a welcome sight to bomber crews on their way back to base.)

Little Massingham is on the northern edge of the village. The church of St Andrew has a square embattled tower. The whole is quite small but of perfect proportions and, in the authors' opinion, one of the most beautiful in Norfolk. Inside is a fine marble and Caen stone pulpit which was added in the 1850s and designed by an architect from Norwich, Mr Jeckel.

Walking up over the A148 – take care as traffic can be ferocious – and adjacent Harpley Dams leads to a delightful section of the Way where all you may encounter on the even surface are rabbits and birds. Watch out, though, for the dozens of marl pits. Marl was dug and added to fields as a general purpose 'improver' 200 years ago and you will see what appear to be their abandoned sites, now shallow depressions in the land or around clusters of trees. Intriguingly, some of these will, on closer inspection, turn out to be Bronze Age tumuli – the sites are protected and the absence of any kind of farming activity around them will provide the best clue as to their origins.

Houghton Hall and Britain's first Prime Minister

You will edge Houghton Hall estate as you head northwards.

Houghton Hall is well worth a prolonged visit if you have the opportunity. It was the home of Sir Robert Walpole, Britain's first Prime Minister, and is a fine Palladian house, Grade 1 listed, set in 100 acres of parkland. Palladian houses generally had plainish exteriors but plush interiors and this is no exception. Silvery-white, restrained and elegant, the house boasts a 5 acre kitchen garden. The estate was designed by Charles Bridgeman and is very largely the same as it was in the eighteenth century.

In the reserve section of the library at Norwich is a fascinating book which was privately printed and issued to subscribers only. It is called *Later History of the Walpole family* and was written by W. Rye in 1920. From this we gain an insight into the sumptuous lifestyle of Sir Robert Walpole at Houghton in a letter of the period : *'From Norfolk they write that Sir R. Walpole keeps an open house at Houghton, so numerous are his attendants and dependants that it is thought his household expenses cannot be less than £1,500 a week.'*

He also is known to have kept greyhounds on a huge scale and we are told that his progress through the county was quite on a regal scale. Upon his return from being made a freeman of Yarmouth, he was met just north of Norwich by the Bishop, Dean and about 1000 clergy and citizens who escorted him home.

Financially, matters deteriorated in succeeding generations until Sir Robert's grandson, the 3rd Earl, was obliged to sell off the world-renowned art collection to Catherine the Great of Russia in order to pay off huge debts.

There are reported to be at least two ghosts at Houghton. One is The Brown or Grey Lady – Dorothy Townsend. She was a young and beautiful girl forced to marry an old man against her will. She was said to haunt the state bedroom and to have frightened George IV when Prince Regent on his visit there. He saw '...*a little lady all dressed in brown, with dishevelled hair and a face of ashy paleness*' by his bedside and he said ' *I will not spend another hour in this accursed house.*' There is another – one of two the brothers who fought a duel in 1620. The loser scours the house looking for revenge on the sibling who killed him.

JUST OFF THE PATH
Sandringham

The path passes within four miles (6.4 km) of the Royal Estate at Sandringham, an ideal and probably more famous excursion.

This royal estate was bought in 1861 for the Prince of Wales by his mother, Queen Victoria. The church of St Mary Magdalene is the home church of Her Majesty Queen Elizabeth II and other members of the Royal Family.

'Dear old Sandringham, the place I love better than anywhere in the world.'
King George V.

This estate has special memories for Stephen, one of the authors of this account . At one time, the top-performing boy each year at his school, King Edward VII Grammar School in Kings Lynn, used to come here to receive a gold medal from King Edward VII himself.

He also remembers as a schoolboy running cross country races around here, hating the racing but never being able to forget the glorious woodland the boys stumbled and splashed through.

The estate is a mixed landscape comprising tidal mudflats, fruit farms, grazing land for livestock, woodland and wetland and makes for a spectacular run.

Regarding the house itself, most of the ground floor rooms used by the Royal Family are open to the public. It is possible for a group to request a time to visit – usually early evening – when they will have the house all to themselves.

Visit www.sandringhamestate.co.uk

There are 60 acres of utterly gorgeous gardens to explore, as beautiful in autumn as in spring and summer. You will never see more fabulous rhododendrons in hues of magenta, lemon, snowy white, pink and lavender. The huge vistas of trees and the vast open skies stir the heart.

You can buy all manner of momentos, but probably the most welcome to walkers will be the freshly pressed apple juice from Sandringham's own orchards.

The road now dips and rises again several times as you pass Fring Cross – there used to be a cross here – and heads into Sedgeford, one and a half miles distant. You will pass the hamlet of Littleport. The trail passes a local landmark, Magazine Cottage, a quite ornate detached affair which was built by the Le Strange family in the seventeenth century to store gunpowder. A local story is that a secret tunnel was built at the same time from the cottage to the local church, St Mary the Virgin.

The land around is rich in history. Between here and Snettisham some fabulous finds in precious metal have been found, most experts agreeing that they are personal adornments dating from the Iron Age. The greatest-ever British find of gold and silver treasure was found here in the 1990s: over 100 torcs (twisted bands of metal – often gold and silver); over 100 gold and silver ingots and over 170 coins dating from the first century AD. Not surprisingly, evidence of metal-working from the Bronze Age has also been discovered.

The church of Sedgeford St Mary is one of 124 churches in Norfolk with round towers.

JUST OFF THE PATH
Castle Rising

Castle Rising lies 7 miles east of the Peddars Way, near the sea, just off the A149. The keep of the castle was built in 1140 by William d'Albini when he married the widow of Henry I, becoming the Earl of Sussex. It is still owned by a direct descendent.

The castle is in excellent condition, bearing in mind its age. A lovely feature is that the grass banks of the castle are host to delicate wild flowers and butterflies in the spring.

This is where Edward II, who was gay, is reputed to have been put to death in an unmentionable way with a red hot poker. It is probably not true, actually, as he was likely smothered, and the deed was done in Berkeley Castle, not here. However, this was where the new King Edward III imprisoned his mother, Isabella, for 28 years having executed her lover, Mortimer, as it was believed that they had both instigated his father's murder. She was known as the 'She-Wolf of France' and is still here, say many. Every full moon a wolf with snow-white fur can be seen prowling the battlements, baying at the moon – this reflects her behaviour in the years leading up to her death in 1358 when, Lady Macbeth-like, conscience ate away at sanity. Yes, well...

The castle itself is very fine – it is probably modelled on Norwich Castle and it, and the ruined church to the north, date from the same period. With walls up to nine feet thick and three storeys high, the castle would have been an impressive sight from the sea. Lynn overtook Rising in importance in the mid sixteenth century and the castle was, for a time, left to rot.

Castle Rising was also, until abolished in 1832, one of the most notorious rotten boroughs in England. This meant that under 900 people – and most of them under the sway of a few powerful ones – could return 2 Members of Parliament at each election. The seats were effectively 'sold' – and you just wasted your money if you tried to contest them. Famous MPs included Samuel Pepys and Sir Robert Walpole, Britain's first Prime Minister and master of Houghton, highlighted above.

Bircham Windmill lies just outside the village of Great Bircham. It is a rare five storey working windmill and has a bakery and tearooms. There is a shepherd's hut available for hire for anyone who would like a break from the path. The owner is Roger Wagg and he is happy to pick up or drop off walkers for a small fee – at time of publication £5. www.birchamwindmill.co.uk

JUST OFF THE PATH
Snettisham

Snettisham is about 3.5 miles off the trail but is a bird-watching site of international importance, with marvellous displays any time of the year.

In winter, wheatears and sand martins can be seen on the beach whilst gulls and terns seek to nest on the dry 'islands'. In summer, avocets and their young chicks seek food alongside oystercatchers, and you may be lucky enough to spot barn owls swooping over the salt marshes in search of food.

Autumn is a noisy time as the Brent geese return en-masse from their breeding grounds to compete for space with literally tens of thousands of waders. Winter sees huge numbers of peregrines and harriers drawn to the saltmarsh. This is also the time to witness one of the most awesome spectacles in the natural world and which has become known as 'the Pink-footed Goose Spectacular '. Just after dawn, from mid-November to late January, tens of thousands of geese fly across the marsh in a V - shaped formation, calling to each other as they go. At dusk they return. You can join a 'Big Pink Breakfast' to witness this wonder if you do not mind getting up very early. Organised by the RSPB – please check their website for each year's exact timings – the cost is only a few pounds and you can also have, at extra but reasonable cost, a sumptuous breakfast at a local restaurant (vegetarians catered for).

> **JUST OFF THE PATH**
> **Heacham**
> To the west is Heacham, now famous as the UK lavender-growing centre but lavender production was once based at Fring.
>
> Heacham probably dates back several thousand years before Christ. It is famous now for its lavender fields which are known world-wide. The legend of Pocahontas, a Virginia Indian chief's daughter, was partly played out here also, with Pocahontas marrying John Rolfe in 1614. The Rolfes are buried in the village churchyard. Rolfe wrote that he loved Pocahontas but was also motivated by saving a heathen's soul by the marriage. They had a son called Thomas. At the end of her life she became very famous as she travelled around Britain, meeting James I amongst many other famous people. She became ill and died in 1617. Films and books have added to the romantic story to the extent that fact is difficult to separate from fiction.

Lavender and luminous evening light

This is the centre of the lavender growing industry and, in summer, the whole village smells lovely. You can visit a lavender farm and stock up on most welcome gifts for family and friends – everything from lavender soap to lavender plants for the garden.

As the beach faces west and the sun sets over the immense sea, the most memorable and long-lingering sunsets occur, probably only rivalled by nearby Hunstanton. Co-author, Stephen, grew up here and, as a young boy, sang in the choir of the village church for six years. This is a memory of a treasured day:

'I remember a perfect summer's day would be, firstly, paying a visit to the old fashioned sweet and ice cream shop of two elderly brothers, Eric and John, in the village where our ragged band would have a drink of fizzy orangeade into which had been put a square of ice cream. The brothers would give us kids both a straw and a spoon and let us sit in the shop and devour this luscious concoction. Any excess change would be spent on blackjacks, fruit salads and pink sherbert flying saucers. Then, pockets bulging, we would wander up to the beach for a swim, ending the day bewitched by the orange, pink, silver and green 'highway of light' as the sun slowly – very, very, slowly – sank over the vast inland ocean. Summer days seemed so wonderfully long then!'

This part of the trail ends in Sedgeford. The farmland in this part of Norfolk produces wheat, sugar beet and barley.

The village is perhaps best known today because of the Sedgeford Historical and Archaeological Research Project (SHARP) which began in 1996 and is one of the largest archaeological projects in the UK all of which actively encourage the participation of volunteers. You can become involved in fieldwork, administration or maybe just join one of the tours of the current excavations into middle Saxon to early medieval sites. Most of this takes place in the summer months. See the website http://www.sharp.org.uk

'I lay in bed this morning and watched hundreds of Plover tumbling and wheeling against a pale primrose sky. They flung themselves up into the wind, whirled and danced like leaves in a gale, fell headlong with a swift alternation of wingbeats, abandoned to the sheer joy of those aerial games they know so well how to play.'

Lilias Rider Haggard, author of several celebrated books on Norfolk and daughter of Sir Henry Rider Haggard, author of *King Solomon's Mines*.

Poppies and daisies can be seen on the path.

Holme-next-the-Sea

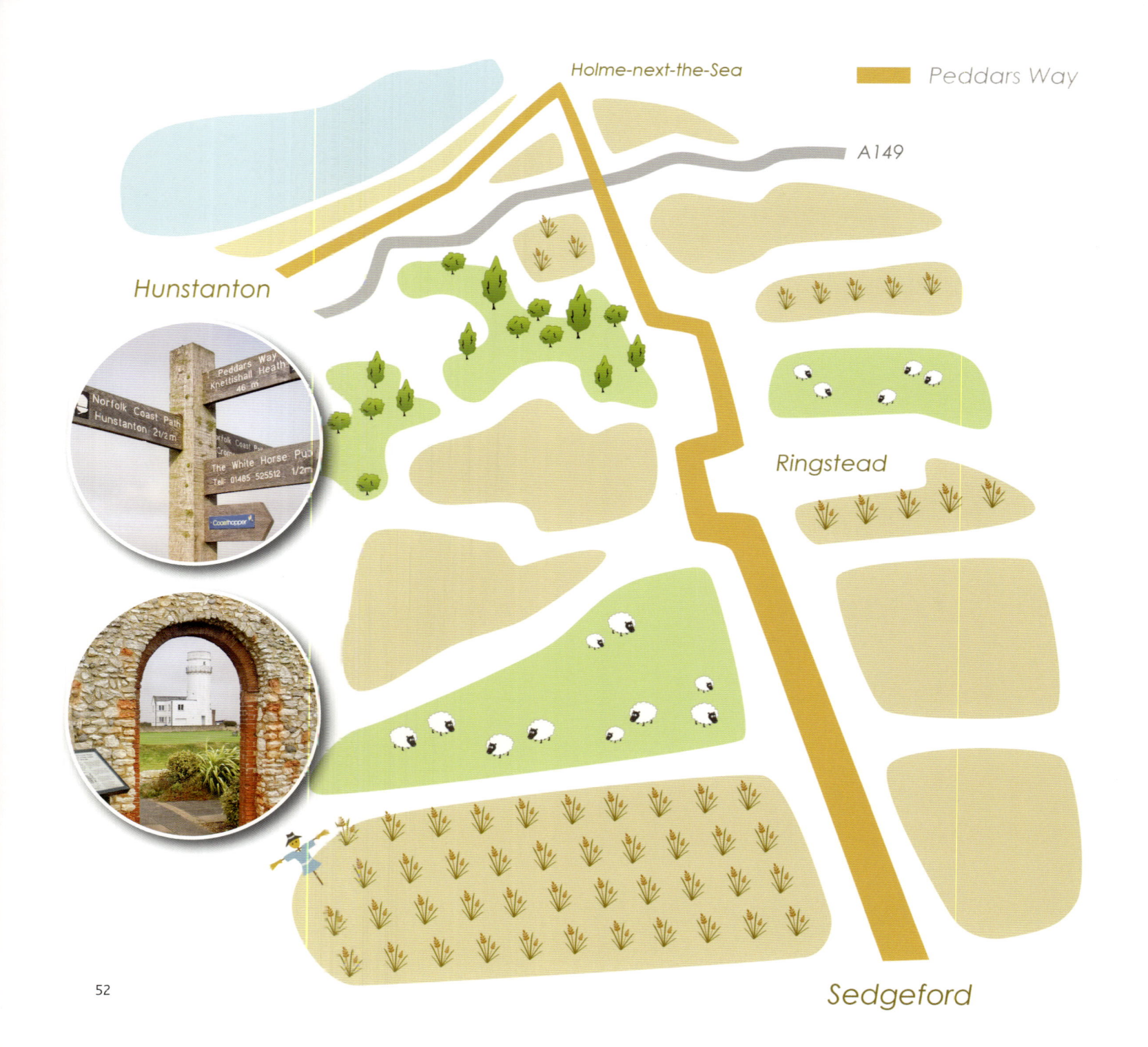

Peddars Way

A149

Hunstanton

Ringstead

Sedgeford

52

Chapter 4
SEDGEFORD TO HOLME AND HUNSTANTON

Distance: about 8.9 miles

'The prevailing wind in Norfolk is onshore; this explains why Norfolkmen invariably speak with their mouths closed.'

Traditional saying.

Section snapshot: This is a very pleasant final section, along mainly green lanes and field pathways, before the Peddars Way meets the Norfolk Coast Path. You can smell and glimpse the vast ocean ahead. You will pass the final Songline sculpture just before Holme. Once at Holme, you will find yourself in a vast wonderland of soft sands, sea pools, dunes and seabirds. The local building material begins to be carstone, with its soft and warm golden light.

Alternative shorter walk: Sedgeford to Holme, 6.25 miles.

Road to Holme.

THE PEDDARS WAY AND NORFOLK COAST PATH

SEDGEFORD TO HOLME AND HUNSTANTON

You will need to rejoin the Peddars Way from Sedgeford. The path goes uphill at first, then over the B1454 before crossing the former trackbed of the old Wells to Heacham railway. At Ringstead, with its houses made from Norfolk Carstone, you become more than ever aware of the sea . On the edge of the village is Ringstead Downs Nature Reserve, cared for by the Norfolk Wildlife Trust. This is a place much loved by people who seek out unusual varieties of wild plants – rock rose and wild thyme for example – as well as being rich in butterflies.

Holme is now about 2 miles ahead. It was here that the Prince of Wales opened the new National Trail in 1986.

A first glimpse of the vast ocean ahead approaching Holme.

Opposite: *A field of rapeseed (*brassica napus*) above the sea at Holme. Rapeseed oil, now the third largest variety by sale of vegetable oil in the world, was first grown here in the nineteenth century and used solely as a lubricant for steam engines.*

Holme-next-the-Sea

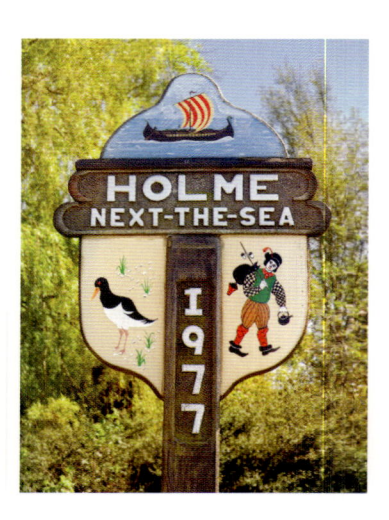

Holme-next-the-Sea, as it is officially known, is perfect for rambling with a good variety of footpaths marked through and along the village. Do try, also, to take a look at the church of St Mary which looks as if it had the various parts have been taken from elsewhere, at different periods, and 'bolted' together. The overall effect is pleasing, though, and it is difficult not to smile as you ponder the purpose of a particularly eccentric memorial or oddly-placed window.

Many of the houses are extremely attractive being built of a mix of Carr stone and clunch – a hard chalk – and often combined with flint.

Holme has a particularly interesting claim to fame – as the 'moth' capital of England. The wind is responsible for the incredible variety – some 500 macro species and 400 micro species have so far been recorded – of moths which land around the town. A flourishing local moth-appreciation society welcomes new enthusiasts. Common are the privet, poplar, lime and eyed hawkmoths. Some, like the bee-hawk or humming-bird moths feed while in flight, their wings beating at such a rate as to render them invisible as they hover over rhododendrons, valerian or honeysuckle. New species are being discovered all the time and some names are

Lantern slide of Holme in about 1900. The houses are made of clunch, Carr stone and flint (reproduced with permission, Picture Norfolk Library).

Right: *The air becomes moist and misty as you approach the Holme Dunes and sea.*

SEDGEFORD TO HOLME AND HUNSTANTON

Evidence of concrete war defences still lie on the coast in this area.

A magical mosaic in the sand bears witness to the migration of millions of pink footed geese every year in late autumn.

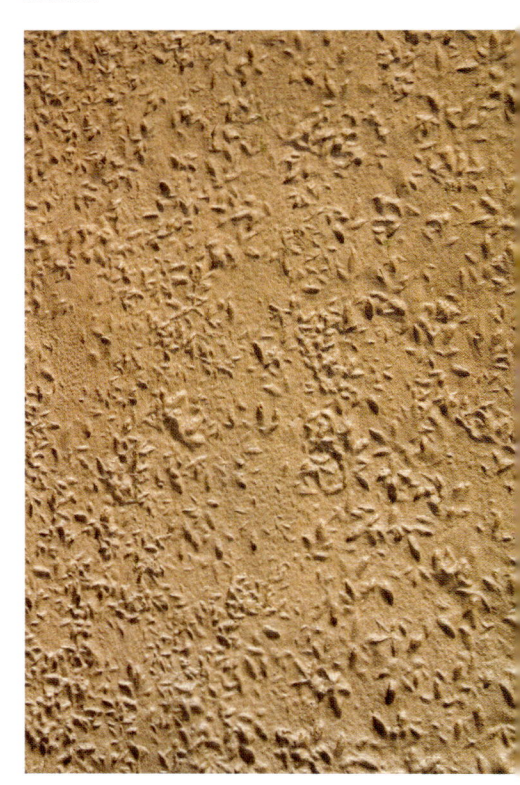

wondrous – convolvulus, oleander, bedstraw, death's head, pale tussock, white satin, reed tassock, emperor and white ermine, to give a few examples.

This may be a good time to talk a little about the butterflies of Norfolk. We have the spectacular yellow and black swallowtail which feeds on carrot and angelica but has a special preference for the milk parsley plant and for this reason is almost never found outside the county. Its caterpillar cannot be mistaken – brilliant green with black stripes and orange spots. You may see the large metallic looking large copper but this is rare in the extreme. Sometimes the Norfolk coast will be full of vast numbers of common whites being blown over the cliffs from the continent like a massive ticker-tape display. Others coming to us in the same way include clouded yellows and the beautifully coloured painted ladies. Less common is the Camberwell Beauty with its black velvety sheen and white or cream borders to the wing. It was first noticed in the mid eighteenth century when it gained the name 'white petticoat'. It is partial to decaying fruit and garden flowers. Finally, although you may well see very many varieties, we must just mention the beautiful red admiral which again is not completely indigenous to our shores, large quantities being blown over from the continent.

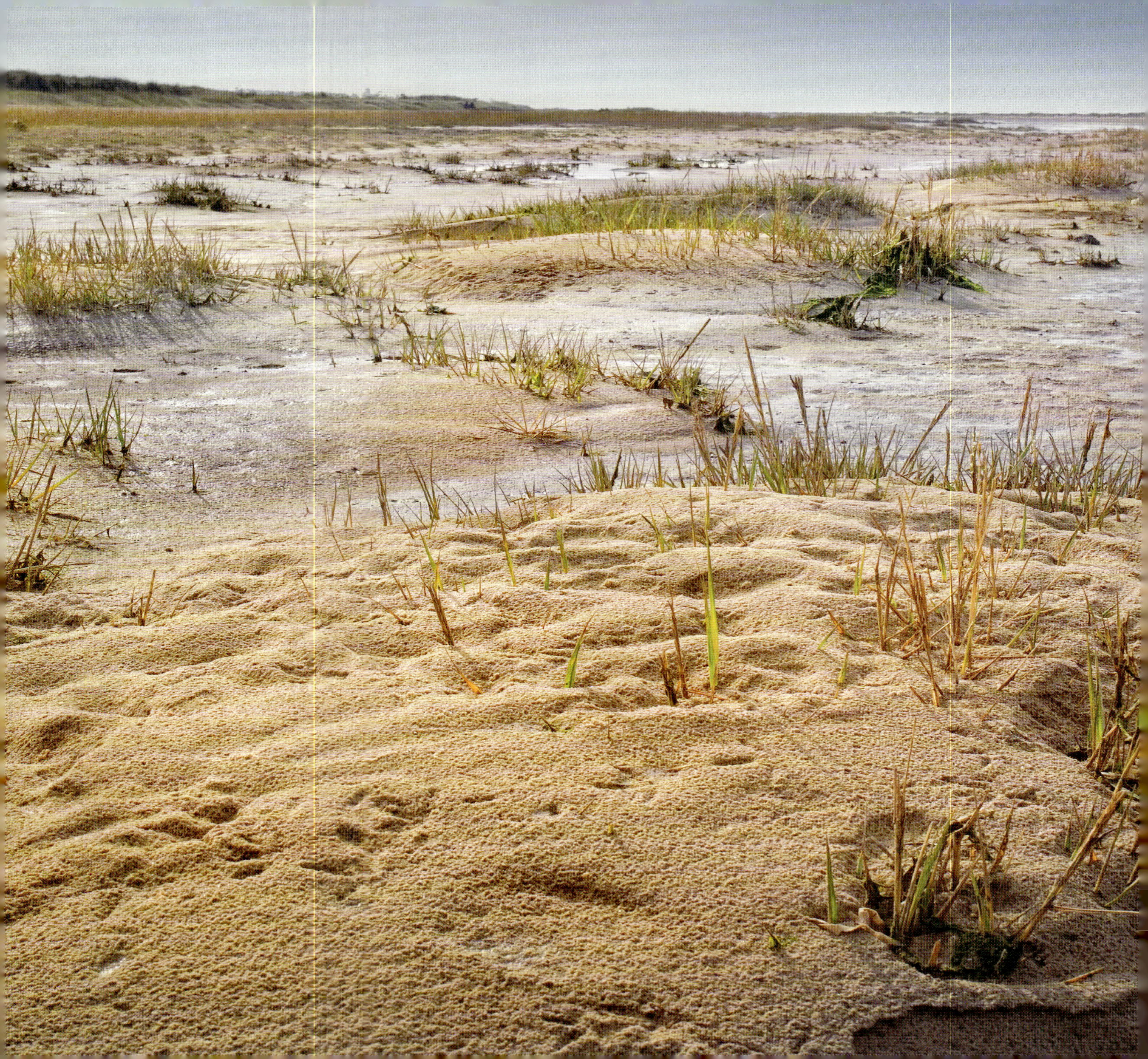

Views of Holmes Dunes – huge flat golden sands, wild grass, pools and sea.

Many of us will have gazed in awe, too, at the beauty of the dragon fly. The identification of these magnificent creatures is an ancient and complex business. Some species are the Norfolk aeshna, the Norfolk coenagrion, symnpetrum and the black-lined orthetrum.

Holmes Dunes and Norfolk Wildlife Trust Nature Reserve

In 1965 the Holmes Dunes National Nature Reserve was created and now covers 550 acres. Apart from moths, butterflies and birds, the reserve is rich in plant life, including marsh orchid and sea lavenders. You can park next to the Holmes Dunes for a couple of pounds - there are a few 'free' places, too, for cars just off the road if you get there quickly enough!

As you wander over the dunes you will witness a quite extraordinary sight – soft golden sands spreading almost as far as the eye can see into an ocean that extends to the horizon. Here there are pools and meandering stretches of water left by the tide as it recedes, sea plants in shades of yellow, soft purple, green and gold, and waders, avocets and little terns. High in the sky above, you may be lucky enough to see vast flocks flying in formation. Sometimes, you become aware of a sense of complete silence and, looking up, realise that although your eyes

Sea thistle on the beach late autumn.

This sign as you approach the sea at Holme marks the end of the 46 mile trail of the Peddars Way and the beginning of the Norfolk Coast Path.

can see for miles in each direction, there is not another human being around.

Dogs are allowed into this walking paradise sometimes but please check before coming – there is a Visitors' Centre serving the reserve which is open every day from April to October and at weekends from November to March.

There is Bird Observatory – to view some of the 382 recorded species – with a warden and nature trail. At some times of year, you can spot enormous flocks of Brent geese, shore waders, chats, greenshanks and sea birds.

The dunes are very popular with all ages, although some of the pools on the sands are deceptively deep. It is also possible to get so carried away exploring the sands and amazing variety of seashells, plants and fungi that you look up in consternation to realise that the sea and sands have shifted. As with all other areas of this coastal trail, it is vital to check the times of the tides before setting out.

In autumn the area of the coast between Holme and Holkham becomes a Mecca for a rapidly-growing band of fungi-spotters. Of course, knowing what it is safe and what is not is the key! Tours to get you started on this fascinating subject are organised at minimal cost by naturalengland.org.uk

Seahenge

In 1998 a circular wooden structure, christened 'Seahenge' by the press, was discovered. It consists of 55 split oak trunks. It has been possible to date the wood accurately to the twenty-first century BC. It has even been possible to establish the number of different axes used in the construction – over 50 – as each left an individual mark. Between 16 and 26 individual trees were used, the central stump being 167 years old when it was felled. Modern science is wonderful in what it is able to establish accurately.

The excavation and preservation of the site has been extremely difficult due to the tides and the opposition of many local people. A good many residents – including the Druids – hold passionate opinions as to what it is right to excavate and what should be left alone. The timbers were eventually taken away for preservation work in spite of protests and a recreated Seahenge can now be seen in the Lynn Museum in Kings Lynn.

The purpose of Seahenge remains a mystery.

This walk takes a 2½ mile 'backward step' here in order to reach Hunstanton.

Going 'backwards' to Sunny Hunny

Long-distance walkers will encounter a trail leading up to the top of the cliffs at Old Hunstanton. However, if you fancy a shorter walk, you can drive to the vast car park at the beginning of Lighthouse Close and progress on foot along the clifftop to New Hunstanton. There are toilets here as well as a café. Look back for unforgettable views of the sand dunes just discussed.

The famous Hunstanton cliffs and shore showing the wreck of the trawler Sheraton *which, over the years, has taken on the appearance of concrete.* Sheraton *was built in 1907 and served in both World Wars before being wrecked in a storm in 1947.*

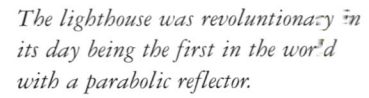

The lighthouse was revolutionary in its day being the first in the world with a parabolic reflector.

The lighthouse, built 1840, seen through the arch of St Edmund's Chapel. Photograph: Stephen Browning

There is a cute roadtrain that operates from here to the new town and back again – very popular with kids but it takes anybody! – and you can ride it either way (picks up by the green at the new town).

The white lighthouse you see straight ahead was built in 1840, although there have been structures with a similar purpose on this spot since at least 1665. The present lighthouse was the world's first with a parabolic reflector. Nowadays, the building serves as holiday lets.

The legend of St Edmund

A few yards away on the green cliff top are the remains of St Edmund's chapel, alongside which is a wooden sculpture of a baying wolf.

St Edmund, the first Patron Saint of England, arrived in this locality as a very young man and was crowned King of East Anglia in 855. For some years he was a benign and just ruler before being defeated by the invading Danes led by a man called Ivar the Boneless at a place

The baying wolf sculpture and the old lighthouse on a misty autumnal morning.

St Edmund and the wolf (see text) naturally feature on the colourful town sign. The motto roughly translates as 'It is our pleasure to please others'.

– exact location unknown – called Haegelisdon. He was offered his life if he denounced Christianity, which he refused to do. He was tied to a tree and his body shot through with arrows (there are obvious parallels with the legend of St Sebastian here) and he was decapitated. His mortal remains were unceremoniously dumped in a nearby wood.

When the broken-hearted people of East Anglia heard of this, they organised a search party for their king, finding his body quite quickly. However, as they could find no trace of his head, one of them yelled out 'Where are you?' Where are you?' A cry came back from further inside the wood: 'Hic, Hic, Hic' (Hic is Old English for 'Here'). The head was found, protected by the forelegs of a wolf. The wolf allowed the head to be taken and went with the men to the body of Edmund where the head miraculously reconnected itself to his body. The wolf returned to the forest.

Follow the path along the cliff top towards New Hunstanton, along Cliff Parade. As you walk looking over the cliffs, you will see not one, but up to four fences, each about a yard further in, stopping any further progress toward the cliff edge. The council has simply put up a new fence each time erosion has impacted the cliffs, leaving the 'old' one in situ. The fact

SEDGEFORD TO HOLME AND HUNSTANTON

The cliffs are spectacular with three coloured layers of rock. They are relentlessly battered and undermined by the waves with some parts in a state of imminent collapse.

Hunstanton shoreline.

THE PEDDARS WAY AND NORFOLK COAST PATH

The Golden Lion Hotel, originally The Royal Hotel, was the first building to be built in Hunstanton new town and for a while was referrred to as 'Le Strange's Folly.

that they are all in reasonable condition still is a physical reminder of just how quickly the land is being eaten away.

As this is an area of sometimes blanket mists, the grass can become surprisingly wet and waterproof footwear is a must. Some walkers choose to use the pavement on the further side of the road.

You will soon pass the area of new houses and flats designed with a sea view. On the left, the buildings become grander, constructed of beautiful deep sandy coloured 'honeystone'. This is the start of the 'New' Hunstanton, designed as a complete new settlement by a celebrated Victorian architect, William Butterworth, and paid for by a consortium of wealthy businessmen led by Henry Styleman Le Strange. You will pass two elegant squares – Lincoln and Boston – which were based on London squares but each having a wonderful sea view. The town was begun in 1846 and linked to Kings Lynn by a new railway.

Opposite: Walking along the cliff top towards the new town, the first building of which is the one with the pointed 'turret' appearance on the left.

'In so many places one regrets the modernisation because it is so infectious.'
Hugh Meredith, referring to Hunstanton, or 'Sunny Hunny' to the locals.

66

The road passes the old 'pitch and putt' course on your right and leads to the Green, the epicentre of the town. Look up to your left to see the very first building ever built here, now called The Golden Lion Hotel. Glance around to witness a wonderful triangle of deep sandy-coloured honeystone buildings, with the bottom side of the triangle being the seafront and promenade. The sixties and seventies have a great deal to answer for here as, especially from the apex and along the right-hand side of the triangle, much quick 'adding on' has been done in order to turn the original buildings into shops and cafés. If, however, you can blot these out in your mind's eye, it is possible to travel back in time and see this town as the beautiful and highly praised settlement it was. The great and the good all came here along with the 'ordinary folk' who utilised the railway.

If you have time, take a walk around the town. To do this, pass upwards to the right hand upper side of the green. Turn right, along the cafés and then first left. Follow Le Strange Terrace into Westgate and turn left into the High Street. This higgledy-piggledy street of golden honeystone has much the same atmosphere as it did years ago, although the shops themselves may have changed. At the end, turn left down the hill, left again at the green, until you stand opposite The Princess Theatre. You are on top of the green, where this mini walk began.

> 'Went to New Hunstanton, which in consequence of the Camp and some excursions from the Midlands was a complete Fair, almost equal to the sands of Yarmouth in the height of the season. … The whole place was replete with life, and every available place of refreshment was crowded.'
> Rev Benjamin Armstrong
> 20 July 1874.

THE PEDDARS WAY AND NORFOLK COAST PATH

Personal memories!
If you look behind you, this is precisely the spot where the co-author of this account, Stephen, spent his teenage years. It was in a restaurant with flat above situated on the ground and first floors of one of these beautiful honeystone buildings. It had (has) five floors, the three above, alas, all being empty at the time. Unfortunately, the water tank was at the top and froze constantly in winter. Many was the time that mother and son went up and down, up and down, with hot water!

As you will see, from the top of the town the Green slopes towards the massive Norfolk ocean over which the sun sets in spectacular fashion – Hunstanton is rare in facing west and the sun actually sets over the sea. For up to five or six hours a day, depending on time of year, silver and golden, at times also pink and red, even greenish, 'roadway' – some locals call it the 'pathway to heaven' – stretches to infinity over the waves. When the tide recedes and it is peaceful, scores of seals bask on the sandbanks. This is also a place of mirages: some claim to have seen magical ships and beautiful castles through the fine haze on a summer's day, on the horizon just above the sea.

Local legends and literature
If there is a reasonable wind, there is no better place for windsurfing. Yet, when a gale blows and the sea roars, it is best to take cover – the pier was completely swept away in 1978. King

John is reputed to have lost the Crown Jewels somewhere in the Wash due to a storm of unprecedented ferocity, so somewhere out there may be riches beyond imagination. Some historians think this may have been an early insurance scam, King John having secured the jewels somewhere else ...

Again, legend has it that when St Felix was sailing in the Wash on his way to bring Christianity to East Anglia in 630 AD, his boat became tossed in a storm. The resident beavers came to his rescue and, in gratitude, he granted the chief beaver episcopal status before landing at nearby Babingley: this is why the first Bishop of Norfolk is reputed to have been a beaver.

One of the most celebrated novelists associated with Hunstan is L.P. Hartley. In 1944 he published *The Shrimp and the Anemone* which drew upon his childhood experiences playing among the rock pools below the famous cliffs. Many became aware of him through the book *The Go-Between*, a work immeasurably melancholy and beautiful in almost equal proportions. The famous film of the book, starring Alan Bates and Julie Christie, was filmed in the region. P.G. Woodhouse was another frequent visitor.

A famous building of quite another sort is the Smithdon High School which was designed by Peter and Alison Smithson and opened in 1954. The style of the building – huge expanses of glass, interspersed with steel and brick – has been called 'The New Brutalism'. Some pupils who went there have told us that this construction could mean being baked in summer and having to wear gloves in class in winter to prevent frozen fingers.

The local food speciality is fish and chips, with some claiming that they are the finest in Britain.

Walkers follow the trail down from Old Hunstanton towards the Holme Dunes.

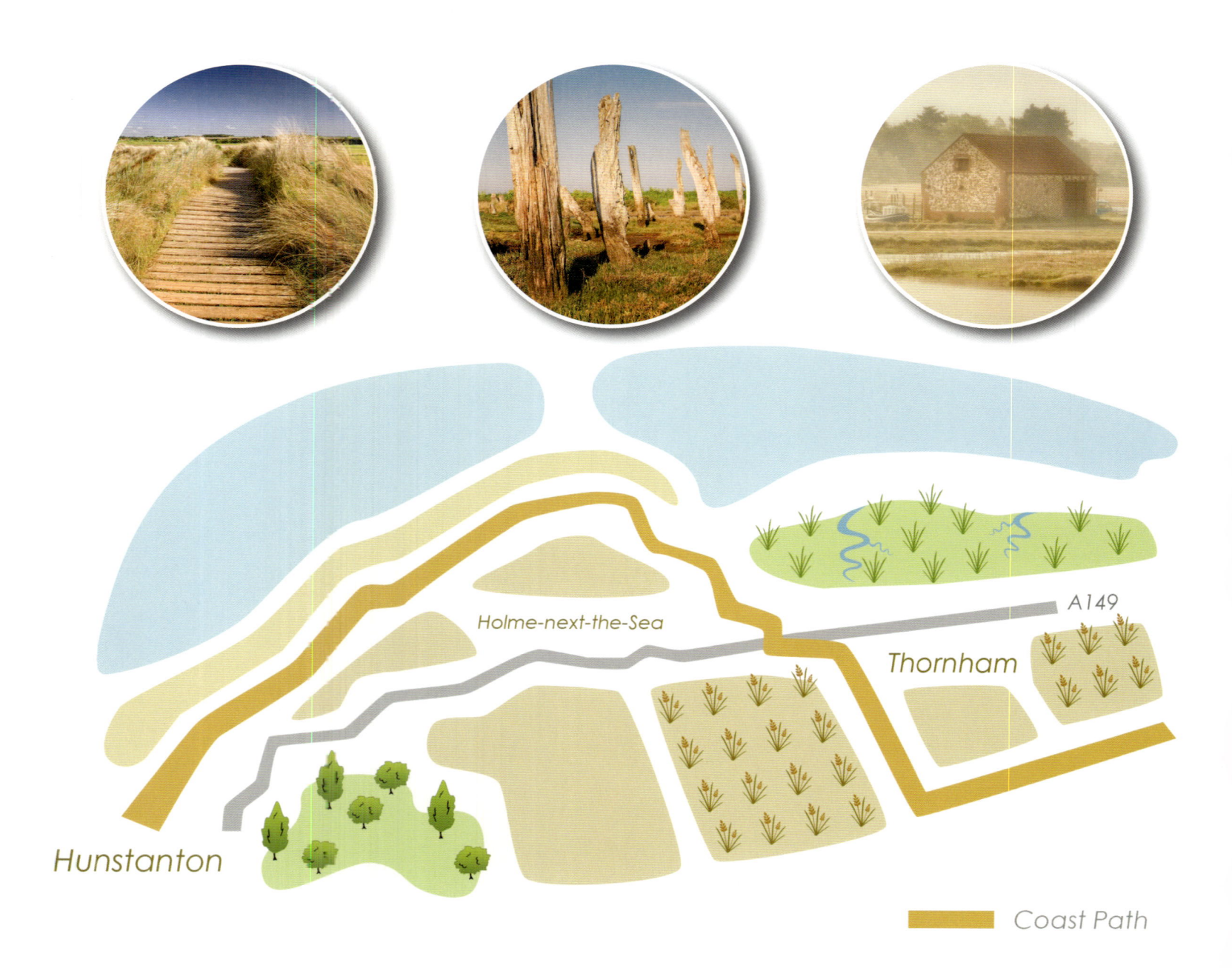

Hunstanton

Holme-next-the-Sea

Thornham

A149

Coast Path

70

Chapter 5
HUNSTANTON TO THORNHAM
Distance: 5.5 miles

'The past is a foreign country; they do things differently there.'
The Go-Between, L.P. Hartley.

Section snapshot: As we are doubling back here, some of the route – particularly in Hunstanton and Holme – has already been discussed. However, as a whole, this is a fascinating walk of many facets, of just under 6 miles from the hustle and bustle of Sunny Hunny through the beauty of Holme to the eeerily lonely and pristine pathways of Thornham. As you exit Hunstanton proper you will gain fabulous views over Holme beach.

Chris and Jenny's story

We met Chris and Jenny while walking the path. We asked them for their impressions of the trail. Did they often walk the trail? Where? Why? They were kind enough to write to us subsequently.

'Jenny in particular works in a very demanding profession and it seemed that we are running just to stand still. We realised that we were working most weekends, although at home we were in different parts of the house. We made a conscious decision to get away at weekends to share and do things together as we used to do our earlier days of courtship and marriage. During our discussions it also became apparent that having comparatively sedentary jobs we weren't very fit.

We lived in Germany for a few years in the early 1980s and went on lots of organised walks with our children. They have many walking clubs there and so lots of choice. It was a wonderful relaxing family experience and we used to look forwards to the weekends, meeting new, interesting people. It was also a great opportunity to practice our German. What we found however, was that somehow the conversation ended up in English as the Germans wanted to practise their English!

We decided to take up walking again - it would aid our fitness, relaxation and give us the opportunity to talk to each other; to share and explore ideas like we used to, and, of course not least, put the world to rights! Longer or long distance walking would ensure that we were away long enough not to be tempted to rush back to complete some task or other that should be tackled in works'

Chris and Jenny Dowden. Jenny is a Headteacher and they live in Downham Market. 10-20 miles a day makes a perfect break at weekends.

The famous Thornham stumps.

time anyway!

Before our decision to take up walking we had met foreign visitors that have explored and were more knowledgeable of the British Isles than we were. So what better way we thought, than to explore some of the long distance National Trails?

We decided to start with the Peddars Way as it was on our doorstep and it would be an easy introduction: after all Norfolk is flat, everyone knows that don't they? Well that is one myth that we have exposed the hard way: as you get further towards the coast the one thing that the Norfolk countryside definitely isn't, is flat!

Several people told us that "The Peddars Way is very boring and really isn't worth the effort!" but when questioned it became apparent that they hadn't been anywhere near it. That was another myth that we were very pleased to expose, and let's face it, like anything in life it's what you make it.

We were very fortunate with the weather, managing the whole trail including the Norfolk Coast Path without one spot of rain. We came across some very interesting creatures some of which we had to look up. We did see a grass snake and an adder, reptiles that I hadn't seen since my childhood growing up in Devon in the 1960s.

The signposting was on the whole very good – there were one or two missing however – but between the Ordnance Survey map and the guide we didn't have any challenges. The guide itself was very worthwhile but what most existing guides **don't** do so well is recreate the 'atmosphere' of the walking. From what you guys have said about your new book, it is very clear that you intend to address this in both pictures and words, and we are very pleased to be involved! There is a very impressive – at times almost overwhelming – 'spiritual' and 'poetic' aspect to the Peddars Way. If you stand still, but not if you rush onward too much, you feel the immensity of this.

The Norfolk Coast Path was quite challenging, as walking on very soft sand dunes even without a heavy rucksack is very demanding on your legs and, of course, slows you down. We did make allowances for the sand but not quite enough and were much wiser after the event. We encountered the same problem walking on the pebbles along the beach part of the path; being round the pebbles had a similar effect to that of the soft sand. We walked this part of the trail in April when there was a storm force easterly gale blowing off the North Sea. The effect was to be sand blasted, especially along the part of the path that tracks along the top of the sea defence wall, leaving us totally exposed; it was so cold we had to wear gloves. Eye protection was essential and we wouldn't have made it without our sunglasses, which we were going to leave behind. (Lucky, lucky!) The coastal path runs through the nature reserve so there was lots of wildlife to observe not least sea birds. At strategic points there were display boards with pictorial information about the wildlife inhabitants. We enjoyed a cup of coffee and cake in the café on Cromer Pier at journey's end and a well-earned rest.'

HUNSTANTON TO THORNHAM

Starting at the Green in Hunstanton, follow the black and white National Trail acorns. You can either experience the fantastic views as you walk on top of the cliffs or, the authors' favourite by a long chalk (many short chalks, too, can be found!) take the track via the seashore looking for fossils and all manner of marine creatures in the sea pools. The most common finds are ammonites – particularly plentiful if you can visit after stormy weather. Here you will gain a fabulous view of the layered cliffs as you look up from the beach.

Thornham is a pretty village and home to just under 500 people, according to the 2001 census. It had about 750 inhabitants in the mid nineteenth century.

All Saints' church is well worth a look. It has had a chequered building history. Originally started in Norman times, building was halted in 1348 due to the Black Death. The tower was left unfinished in 1666 as the master masons were needed to help rebuild London after the Great Fire. By Victorian times it had become severely dilapidated and it took over fifty years to restore. Now it is quite lovely. Especially noteworthy are the carved bench ends, some of which represent poppy heads, anger, drunkenness and sloth. The minesweeper HMS *Thornham* gave its bell to the church in 1969 and it is rung once a year.

The Path at Thornham.

Mists roll over Thornham marshes.

Coast Path

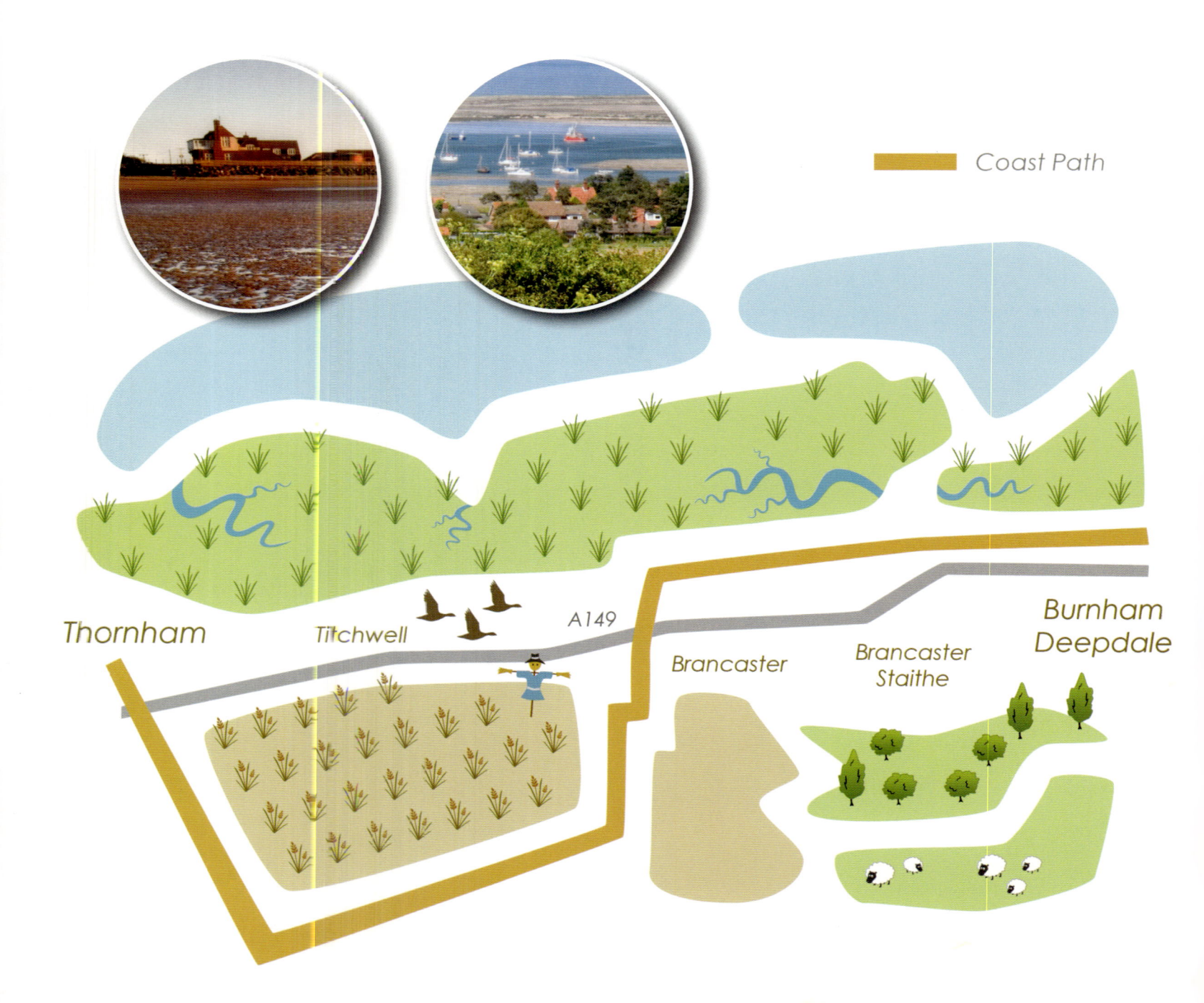

Thornham Titchwell A149 Brancaster Brancaster Staithe Burnham Deepdale

Chapter 6
THORNHAM TO BURNHAM DEEPDALE

Distance: 5.5 miles

'I am a Norfolk man and glory in being so.'
Admiral Lord Nelson who gained his love of the sea as a boy in Brancaster.

'A quiet, happy little corner of Norfolk this.'
Hugh Meredith.

Section snapshot: This is again a varied walk with some awesome views. Start at the Orange Tree in Thornham and follow the black and white National Trail acorns going eastward from there. You will come to the sign for the tiny hamlet of Choseley. The 2011 census shows a population of 18. Choseley drying barns attract birdwatchers who can be rewarded with sightings of rare birds, including the corn bunting. For about a mile you will now be walking on a small road.

Off Thornham beach are signs of a prehistoric forest.

Soon you will see a sign on your left leading to a small copse and then a pleasant slightly slanting track uphill. After a couple of minor road crossings and, following wet weather, some very muddy farm tracks, you will begin a descent into Brancaster. The views here are quite fantastic. This area is popular with birdwatchers and is a good place to take a breather or picnic and take out your bird-indentification book and binoculars.

Once in Brancaster, Choseley Road joins Mill Road and the A149 at the crossroads with St Mary's church. Walk down the narrow lane and take the boardwalk path amongst the reeds, heading to the east.

Brancaster will always have unrivalled historical fame as the place where Britain's greatest sea hero, Lord Nelson, began to mess about in boats. Later, of course, he messed up those of the country's enemies, primarily France and Spain. In his most famous battle, Trafalgar, in 1805, he beat the larger combined fleet of both countries by the unprecedented tactic of

Brancaster is famous for mussels in winter and fabulous fresh beach walks all the year round.

JUST OFF THE PATH
A little off the route, east of Brancaster, is the Roman fort of Branodunum. Branodunum was built in 225-235 AD. Originally it would have been on the seashore and its purpose was to deter aggressors coming into the vast Wash. We are able to discover a good deal about it from what remains and from aerial photography. It was rectangular in shape with rounded turrets at the corners. There was a V shaped ditch to the front and it would have been designed to protect a civilian community.

attacking them in the middle and separating them. He then picked them off, one after another. Twenty of the enemies' ships were sunk and not a single one of the British fleet was lost. It is fascinating to look at the tranquil and beautiful view here and to try to imagine the storm and fury of Nelson's last battle. He was lost, of course, probably because he did not have time to change his flamboyant clothes: awash with medals and easily visible, he was shot by a sniper from an enemy ship. Nonetheless, his heroics at sea, combined with those of Wellington on land ten years later at Waterloo, marked the beginning of the 'high point' of the British Empire – henceforth, for a hundred years, Great Britain was unchallengeable as a world power.

Many believe that Nelson had a premonition that he would die in the battle. This is maybe due to the following extract from a letter he wrote just before he gave the famous command *'England Expects That Every Man Will Do His Duty'* – which, it is reported, many of his men actually resented, being quite prepared to do their duty anyway!

' *Most probably I shall never see Dear dear Burnham again, but I have a satisfaction in thinking that my bones will probably be laid with my Fathers in the Village that gave me birth.*'

Note: He was born just 'down the road' at Burnham.
From *Ballads, Songs and Rhymes of East Anglia* by A.S. Harvey (Jarrold and Sons Ltd, Norwich, 1935).

In the 1950s it was seriously mooted that Brancaster should become the centre for the UK's space programme.

At Brancaster Staithe harbour take the path leading through the fishermens' huts.

Soon you will come to Burnham Deepdale and the Deepdale Farm complex. This is a key stopping-off and refreshment point with a campsite, information centre, shops and café. Buses (Coasthopper) stop off by the car park.

A wreck, once the SS *Vina* and used by the RAF as target practice in 1944, lies visible offshore. Nothing can be done as experts believe that the only way to remove it would be with explosives but so much would be required that the operation may well blow up the windows of the houses on the mainland.

The famous Royal West Norfolk Golf Club is here, opened in 1892. It is unusual in that it was built on common land and so the common folk of the area are entitled to use it. It can flood, too, as it is built on salt marsh and it can be extremely windy.

In Burnham Deepdale itself, St Mary's church has an exquisite and rare Norman font which depicts the farming calendar throughout the year.

James Bond came to Burnham Deepdale in the incarnation of Pierce Brosnan: in *Die Another Day*, the marshes represented a paddy field in North Korea.

Parking should not be a problem as there are car parks at Brancaster Beach and Brancaster Staithe Harbour. There are no specific disabled spaces, though.

Wheelchair users will find the bus companies most helpful but they ask that you please telephone beforehand so that the best advice can be given.

There are no shortage of cafés at Thornham, Brancaster, Brancaster Staithe and Burnham Deepdale.

A useful website for more information is www.brancasterstaithe.co.uk

Was there ever a more beautiful spot to simply sit and look? This seat is on the path at Brancaster Staithe.

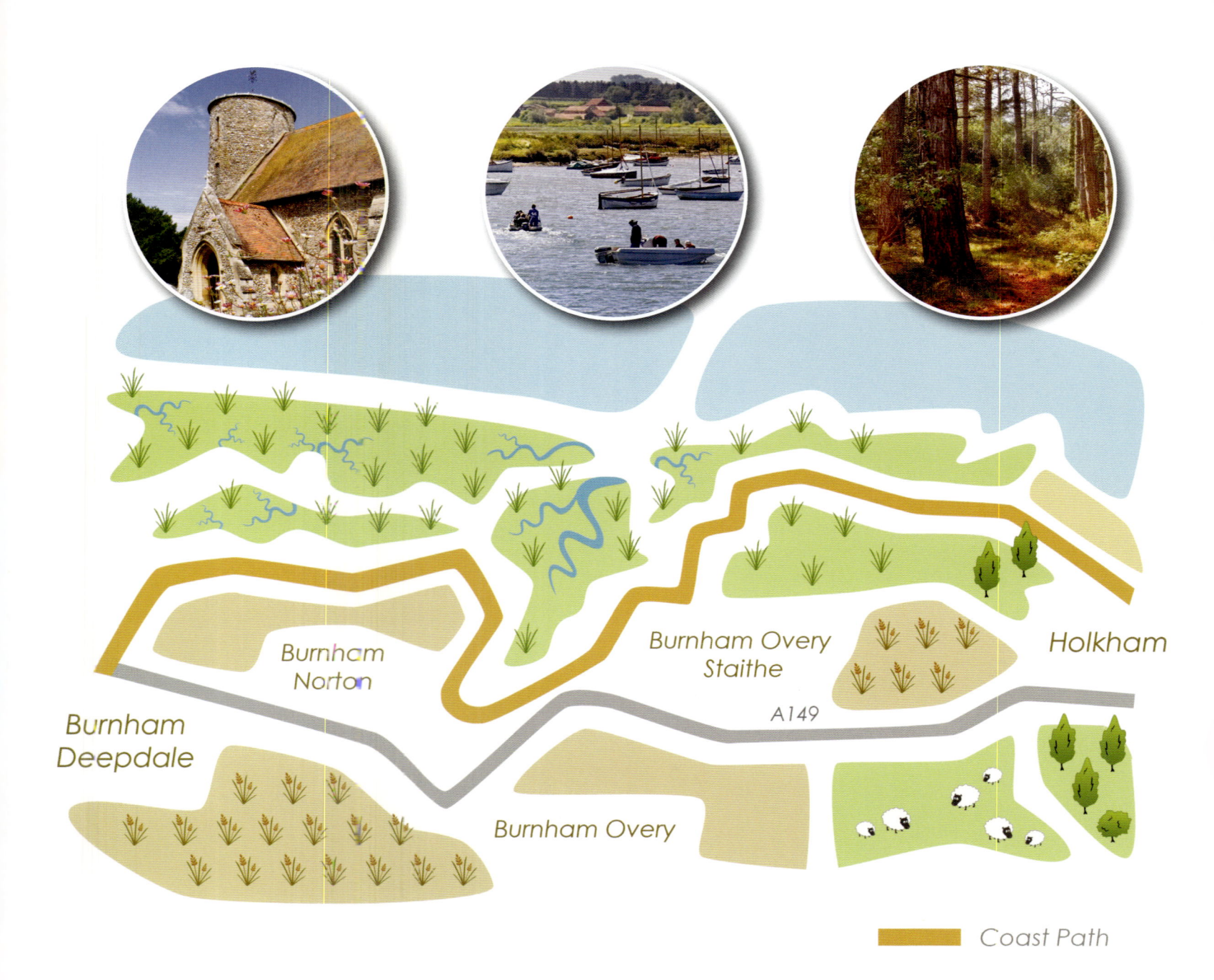

Burnham Deepdale

Burnham Norton

Burnham Overy Staithe

A149

Burnham Overy

Holkham

Coast Path

78

Chapter 7
BURNHAM DEEPDALE TO HOLKHAM

Distance: 8.1 miles

'You either get Norfolk, with its wild roughness and uncultivated oddities, or you don't. It's not all soft and lovely. It doesn't ask to be loved.'
Stephen Fry.

Scenic snapshot. This walk along the floodbanks towards one of Norfolk's most beautiful beaches will most certainly blow away any cobwebs. An extra layer of clothes may be a good idea as it can be very windy.

Follow the black and white National Trail acorns beginning at the Drove in Burnham Deepdale.

Walk the floodbank around Burnham Norton towards Burnham Overy Staithe.

View over marshland at Burnham Deepdale.

THE PEDDARS WAY AND NORFOLK COAST PATH

BURNHAM DEEPDALE TO HOLKHAM

St Mary's church, Burnham Deepdale, is beautiful in proportions but a purist's nightmare – the round tower dates from Saxon times and it has some original medieval glass but the remainder is the result of three major Victorian restorations.

Grounded for good.

Opposite: *Crab pots at Burnham Deepdale.*

THE PEDDARS WAY AND NORFOLK COAST PATH

Dusk gathers on the village of Burnham Overy Staithe.

BURNHAM DEEPDALE TO HOLKHAM

If you are lucky enough to take an aerial trip over this area you will see a number of drainage ditches which date back to medieval times when attempts were made to cultivate the unfriendly soil. More successful probably were oyster beds and salt production – this area was thus probably quite prosperous in post medieval times.

As you come closer to Burnham Overy Staithe you will spot a windmill which dates from 1814. No longer functioning for its original purpose, it is now let as a holiday home.

There are two settlements, Burnham Overy Town – the original (now) small village and the larger Burnham Overy Staithe, about a mile away and next to the harbour. To make things slightly more complex, the 'Town' is about 1 mile from the larger Burnham Market in one direction and Burnham Thorpe, birthplace of Nelson, in the other.

Until about five hundred years ago, ships could navigate as far as Burnham Overy Town, but no longer as the inlet has silted up.

A lovely walk of about one and a half miles leads from Burnham Overy Staithe to the beach.

Walk through the village past the harbour and once again into the floodbank. A ferry may be taken from here to Scolt Head Island. The 'island', so called, is left entirely to nature's whims and natural processes take their due course.

Now a centre for sailing sports of all sorts, Burnham Overy Staithe was, prior to silting up, a major port for the North Norfolk coast. A huge gong would be rung when a ship came in to call the workers in the fields down to the harbour for unloading. The last such activity took place just after the end of the First World War.

THE PEDDARS WAY AND NORFOLK COAST PATH

Flocks of migrating birds over Burnham Overy Staithe marshes.

84

Continue walking on top of the floodbank and enjoy the spectacular views.

Walk onto the beach taking care to keep well clear of nesting birds in spring and early summer. This part of the coast also attracts naturists.

Holkham Estate own this part of the beach and you may well wish to visit the fabulous house and deer park. Much of the present park comprises land that has been reclaimed from the sea. The house itself is an important Palladian structure, built for an ancestor of Thomas Coke who later became the 1st Earl of Leicester. He was very proud of his achievement and, over the main entrance to his hall is the following inscription: *'This seat, on an open, barren estate, was planned, built, decorated, and inhabited in the middle of the eighteenth century by Thomas Coke, Earl of Leicester'*. Nor was this man, destined to convert this desolate area into one of the most productive areas in the country, without a sense of humour. He wrote that, when he first went there, it was no rare thing for *'two rabbits to be found fighting over one grass-blade'*. (Taken from *Norfolk* by W.A. Dutt, first published 1902.)

The present earl lives there now. There is always a great deal going on: see www.holkham.co.uk

Burnham Overy Staithe's name means 'homestead by a stream'.

Further evidence of the prosperity of this part of the coast is provided by numerous middle Saxon pottery fragments as well as extremely fine metalwork which probably came from continental traders. This further suggests trading routes between here and what is now Europe.

This picture gives the view both in front and behind you! On the left is the view of the path leading into Burnham Overy Staithe. If you turn and face the other way, the picture on the right is the path you have just trodden.

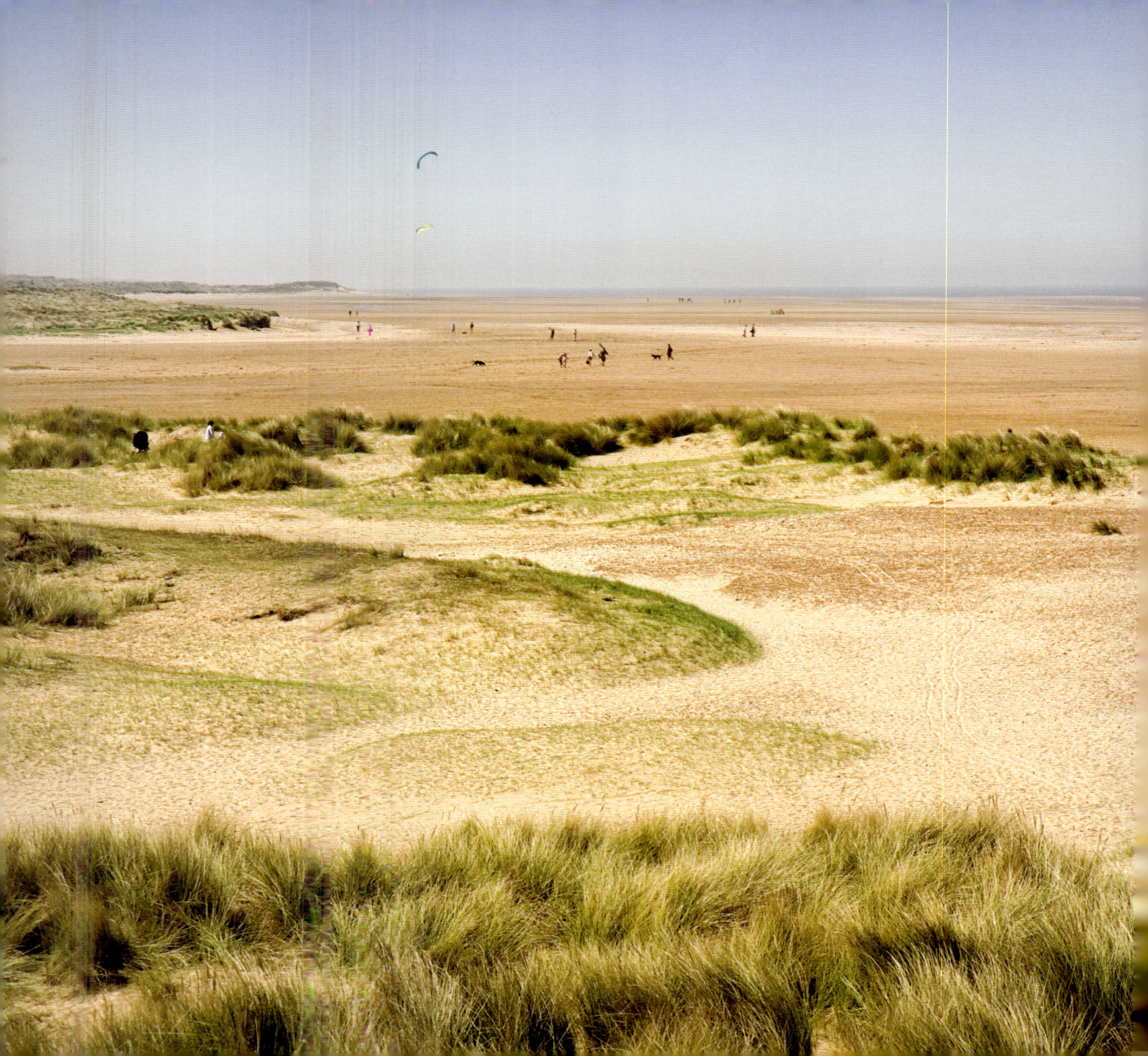

BURNHAM DEEPDALE TO HOLKHAM

Above: *Holkham.*

Left: *The ground is covered with hundreds of thousands of shells at Holkham.*

Opposite: *Holkham Bay.*

Coast Path

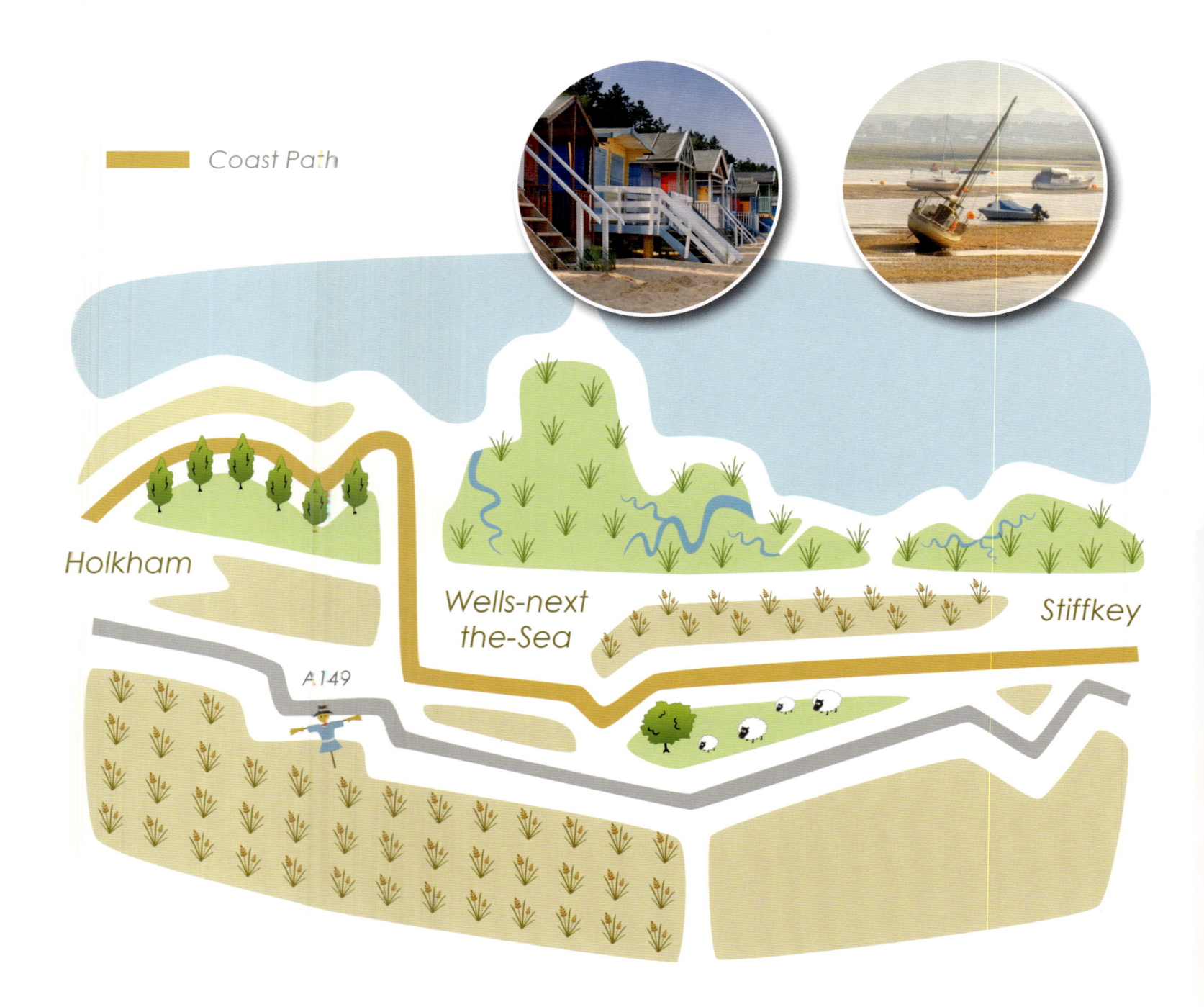

Holkham

Wells-next-the-Sea

A149

Stiffkey

Chapter 8
HOLKHAM TO STIFFKEY

Distance: 7.2 miles

'I have lived in Norfolk all my life. It inspires me, the sea, the limitless skies, the mud and the burning sunsets and the freedom of a place where more than 50% of the neighbours are fish.'

Raffaella Barker, Norfolk novelist.

Section snapshot: This, for many walkers, is the North Norfolk coast at its finest. It is a walk with everything – sandy pathways (with some loose stones), tarmac, floodbank and marvellous fresh air. It can, though, get very muddy following wet weather.

The beach at Wells-next-the-Sea on a perfect summer's day.

An original specially commissioned acrylic painting of Wells-next-the-sea by Daniel Tink (Photographer for this book)

Starting at Holkham, follow the black and white National Trail acorns to the boating lake and car park. Walk up onto the floodbank.

In 1978 the floodbank was breached, washing up onto what is now the play area. The sea bank here now hosts a wondrous variety of wildflowers. You may agree with the late Spike Milligan when he said that wildfowers 'intoxicate with their beauty'.

The town of Wells-next-the-Sea is a picturesque centre with some dazzling panoramas. It is famous for its shellfish.

'The boys from Holt will never bolt,
The Thetford lads are thorough,
And so, I wis, are the chaps from Diss,
Wymondham and Attleboro'.

The Swaffham chaps are good at 'scraps',
The Wells sound as a bell,
And hard as nails are the railway men
From Melton Constable.'

From *The Norfolk Recruit's Farewell* by Cloudesley Brereton (Jarrold and Sons, Norwich 1935).

HOLKHAM TO STIFFKEY

You can walk for 1½ miles along the sandy beach, famous also for its colourful beach huts. Accessible behind the beach are one-hundred-year-old pine woods where you may spot grey squirrels and some rare birds.

The Quay is a favourite spot to eat, either in a restaurant or sitting with fish and chips, cooked crab or crabsticks on the front.

Railway enthusiasts will be fascinated both by the Walsingham Light Railway and the Wells Harbour Railway, both 10 and a quarter inch guage. Kids love to take the train from the town to the beach – they run every 15 minutes. There are four trains now operating and they are called Densil, Weasel, Howard and Edmund.

The town itself has a very elegant green at the centre called The Buttlands overlooked by a couple of comfortable hotels with good restaurants offering locally cooked food. The green itself, like Chapelfield Green in Norwich, was used in past centuries for archery practice, Norfolk boasting the finest battle archers in the Kingdom.

A good website for more information is www.wells-guide.co.uk

The famous and colourful Wells beach huts.

JUST OFF THE PATH

You may wish to take a trip to nearby Walsingham either in the above train or on foot. It has a fascinating history and is still visited by pilgrims from all over the world. Walsingham became a religious centre following a vision by Lady Richeldis, who owned Walsingham Manor, in 1061. The Virgin Mary transported Lady Richeldis to Nazareth where she was shown the place that Jesus was born and instructed to build a replica in Walsingham. There she built a simple wooden structure and afterwards a priory was established. It became very wealthy – in 1511, Erasmus visited and said ' You will say it is the seat of the gods, so bright and shining as it is all over with jewels, gold and silver'.

Henry VIII plundered it in 1538 with the complicity of the Prior, one Richard Vowell, whose reward was a pension to the vast tune of £100 per year. A poem of the time lamented:

Levell levell with the ground
The Towers doe lye,
Which with their golden glitt'ring tops
Pearsd oute to the skeye.

Where weare gates noe gates are new,
The waies unknown,
Where the presse of freares did pass,
While her fame far was blowen.

Oules doe scrике where the sweetest himmes
Lately wear songe,
Toades and serpents hold their dennes
Where the palmers did throng.

Weepe. Weepe, O Walsingham,
Whose days are nights,
Blessings turned to blasphemies,
Holy deeds to dispites.

Sinne is where our lady sate,
Heaven turned is to helle;
Satan sitthe where our lady did swaye'
Walsingham, O farewell!'

The site lay in ruins until 1897 when it was restored, and a replica of Lady Richeldis' shrine was erected in 1931. Today, as we say above, it is once again a place of pilgrimage for many.

Awaiting the tide at Wells.

The saltmarsh to your east boasts some of the most varied wildlife in Europe. You will glimpse waders in the more remote parts spots – oystercatchers, red-legged redshanks, and little egrets, the latter having taken a shine to the area in recent years.

You will see a circle of hardstanding called the Whirligig which was used during the Second World War to test miniature surveillance aircraft. The saltmarsh itself is really a 'no-go' area as it can be very dangerous, so it is vital to stick to the pathway.

Once you reach the National Trust car park, follow route towards the village of Stiffkey. The Coasthopper stops here (on the A149 coast road).

There is a rare circular World War One pillbox just off High Sand Creek camp site.

Holkham National Nature Reserve runs from Burnham Norton to Morston and is approximately 4000 hectares in total, Holkham Bay being the epicentre.

It was reported in 2011 that a rare species of ant-lion, *Euroleon nostras*, had been discovered in the area. The banks of sand are perfect for their homes. Almost 2000 larval pits of this ferocious predator were subsequently found. Adults resemble small dragon flies but are actually of members of the lacewing family. They feed on ants, woodlice and other invertebrates, which wander over the rim of their cone-shaped burrow and fall into the ant-lion's huge jaws where they are sucked dry. For two years they live in this way before becoming flying adults, surviving only about a month thereafter.

Tea rooms, cafés, fish and chip shops and/or pubs are available at Holkham, Wells and Stiffkey. There are several public toilets. The Norfolk Coast Path in general is served with extensive facilities as compared to almost none at all in some earlier sections of the walk. If you are not sure if walking is for you, then it can be a good idea to take one of the shorter walks which we outline on the coast as diversions and resting places are readily at hand if necessary!

Blakeney Point

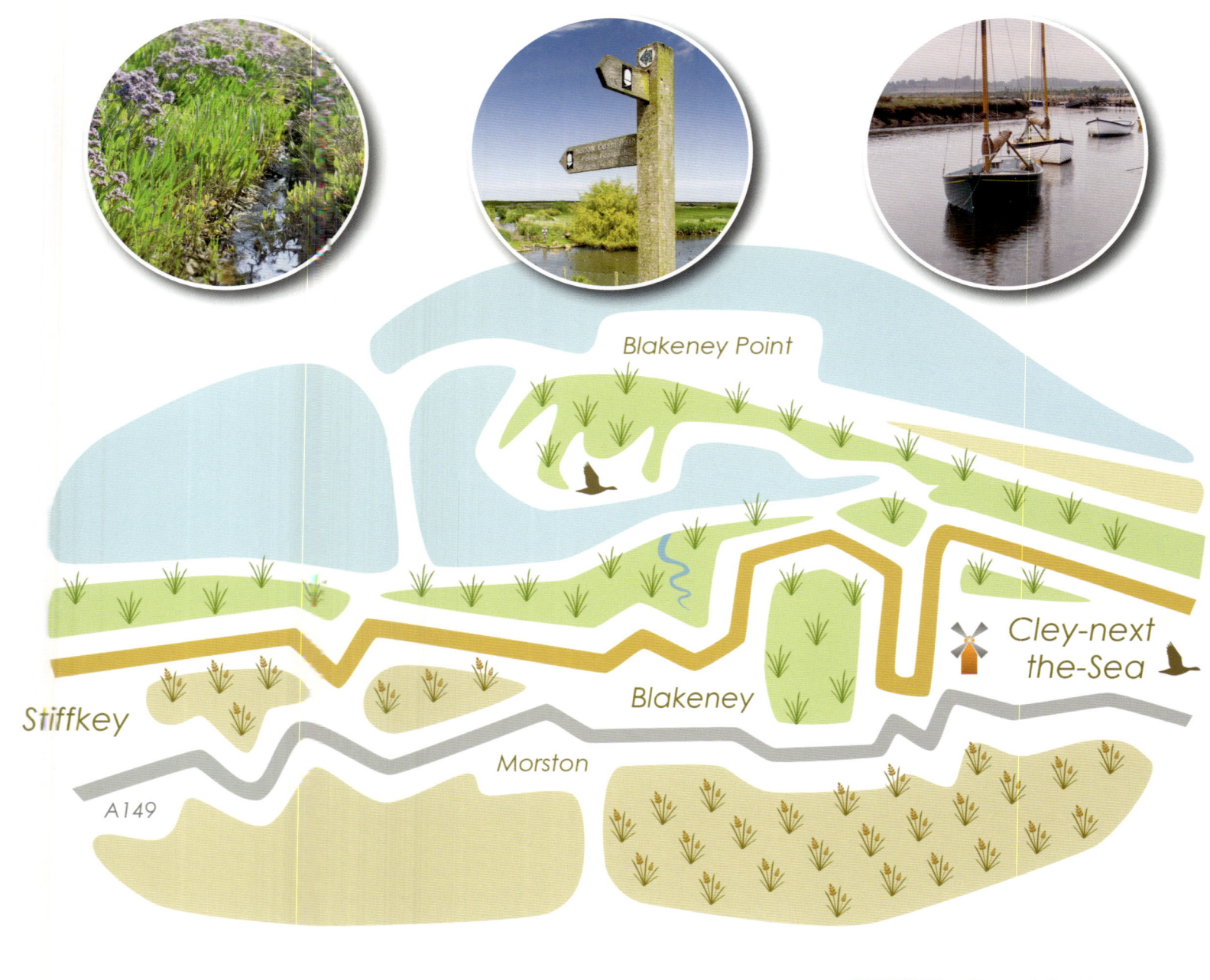

Stiffkey

Blakeney

Morston

A149

Cley-next-the-Sea

Coast Path

94

Chapter 9
STIFFKEY TO CLEY

Distance: 6.5 miles

'Oh! Rare and beautiful Norfolk.'
John Sell Cotman (1782-1842) Leading member of the Norwich School of artists.

Section snapshot: This walk is unforgettable for views over the saltmarsh and for birdlovers. Binoculars, cameras and perhaps sketch books are a must.

This walk takes you past the villages of Stiffkey and Morston, and through Blakeney to Cley.

A thousand years ago Morston was called 'Merstuna' – literally 'farmstead by the marsh'. Stiffkey means 'island with stumps of trees'.

Stiffkey from the Path.

THE PEDDARS WAY AND NORFOLK COAST PATH

Views of Stiffkey from the Path.

The extraordinary life and terrible death of Harold Davidson, Rector of Stiffkey

Summary: Harold Davidson was born in 1875. He became Rector of Stiffkey but was defrocked for immorality in 1932. He died after being savaged by a lion in Skegness in 1937.

Davidson came from a church family and could count an Archbishop of Canterbury among over two dozen clerical relations. He was not overly academic, having been asked to leave Exeter College, Oxford as he preferred to be elsewhere most of the time and failed his exams. He was, however, a powerful speaker and a deeply principled man, gaining the lifetime support of the Bishop of London with the result that his clerical career went very well, indeed – at least initially. In 1906 he gained a fine appointment as Rector of Stiffkey St John with Stiffkey St Mary Morston where he administered all the land owned by Marquess Townshend. He was diminutive in stature at just 5 foot 3 inches, but full of energy and much loved by his parishioners, all of whom he sought to know and visit. His future looked golden.

He had, however, if not exactly a secret, well at least something it was wise not to shout about in this highly prudish age – he used to visit prostitutes in Soho, London, helping them in any way he could – sometimes giving them money but more often arranging them to gain employment. Later at his trial, it did not bode well for him as it was revealed that this employment was usually in the theatre, which was seen as a den of vice. In reality, he had many contacts there because he had been keen on the stage since his undergraduate days. He also made one or two serious enemies as he saw himself not as a man to hold his tongue unnecessarily. One person, in particular, could not stand him – a Major Philip Hamond who owned land in Morston. The Rector had refused to allow the Major to be churchwarden and they had several other altercations.

In 1930 the Rector missed Remembrance Day Service and he was accused by Major Hamond of insulting the dead. It did not help that the rector kept quiet about the reasons for his absence which may well have been because he was delayed from returning from his work with the Soho prostitutes.

In what sounds remarkably similar to the persecution of Oscar Wilde several decades previously, Major Hamond gained wind of the Rector's London 'mission' and made a charge of immorality against him which, if proved, would lead to defrocking. A private detective agency was engaged in London to follow the Rector. Of 40 girls who were approached, only one had anything dishonourable to say about Davidson and this was when she was drunk: when sober, she recanted and subsequently tried to commit suicide.

However, the wheels of ecclesiastical law had begun and Davidson was sent for a Church disciplinary trial which began on 29 March 1932. On 8 July the Rector was found guilty on all charges.

His life became even more bizarre. In September of the same year he appeared fasting in a barrel in Blackpool. He would also appear being roasted and prodded by the 'devil' with a pitchfork. Finally, in 1937, the Rector appeared in an amusement park in Skegness where he shared a cage with a lion and lioness all the while bemoaning his fate. On 28 July he stood on the tail of the lioness and was attacked by the lion.

He was buried in Stiffkey, thousands gathering to pay their respects. The case of Harold Davidson, the Rector of Stiffkey, sometimes known at the 'Prostitutes Padre' remains the subject of fascination right up to the present day. It has been the subject of several plays, films, novels and even a musical. As to his guilt or innocence, the jury is still out.

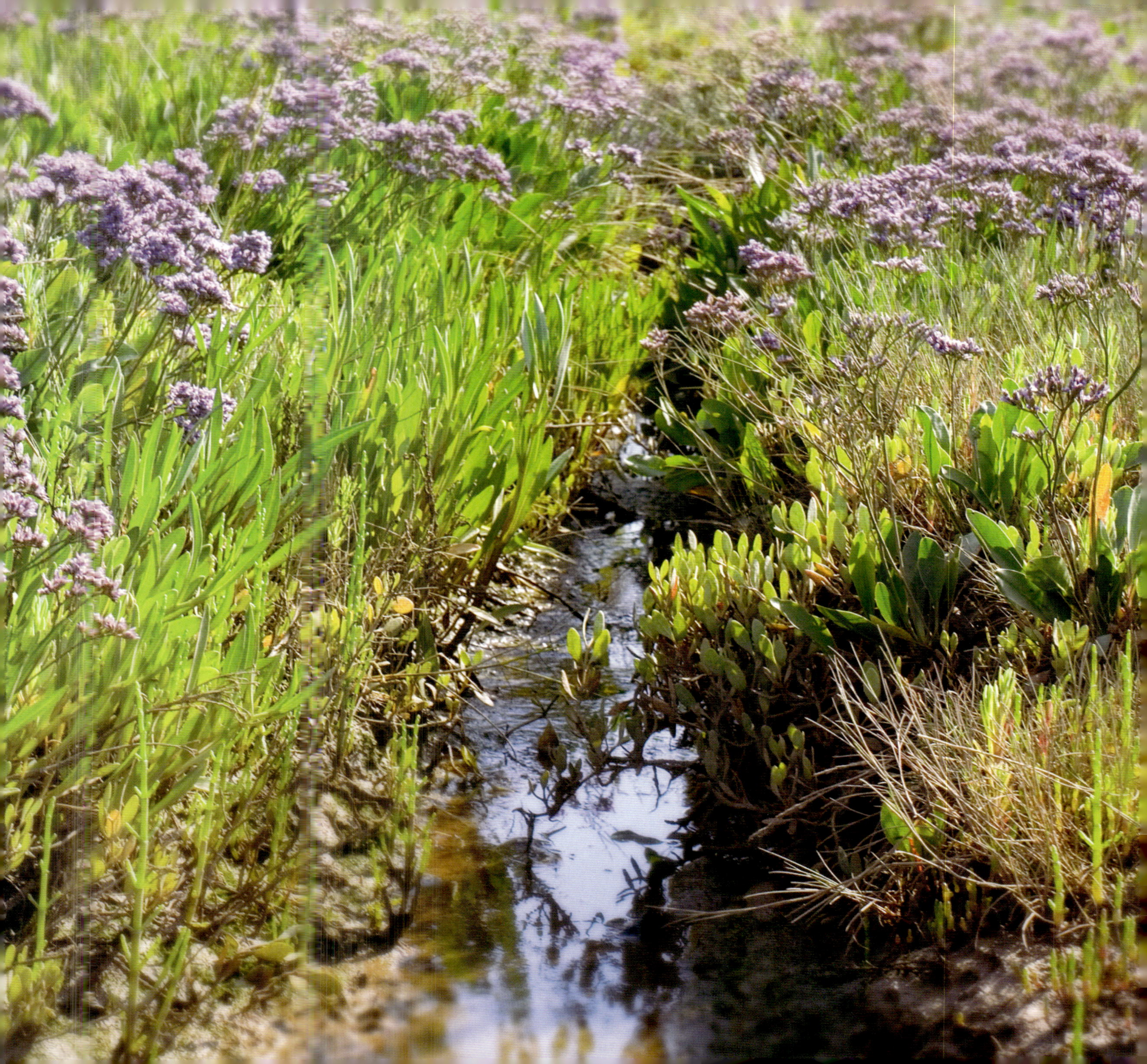

Past famous residents include Henry Williamson, author of *Tarka the Otter*. He bought Old Hall Farm in 1937 but eight years later the farm failed and he moved to Devon.

Binham Priory

South of Stiffkey (on the Norfolk Coast Cycleway) is Binham Priory, a most impressive set of monastic ruins, initially founded by Pierre de Valognes and his wife, Albreda, just after the Norman conquest. Pierre was the nephew of William the Conqueror. The nave now serves as the parish church. Originally a Benedictine priory dependent on the Abbey of St Albans, it originally housed eight monks but we know that when it was suppressed in May 1539, this number had fallen to six. The priory must have been reasonably wealthy because it received the tithes from thirteen churches on land also given to Pierre.

A tunnel is said to run from the priory to an unknown destination. Some years ago, legend has it, a fiddler and his dog decided to investigate. The people at the entrance heard him for some time but then silence fell: he and his dog were never seen again.

The church at Morston is mosty thirteenth century, the tower being a little of a hotch-potch after it was hurriedly repaired after being struck by lightening in 1743.

Once, the villages of Blakeney, Cley and Wiveton comprised the Glaven ports, around the mouth of the River Glaven. During the medieval period Blakeney was a nationally noted port and Cley was indeed 'next the sea' which it is no longer. The whole area gradually became silted up and thus home to the many varieties of birds that can now claim the saltmarshes as home.

There is rumoured to be a monastery which has sunk under the marshes.

Blakeney Guildhall, the grand house of wealthy merchants in the fourteenth or fifteenth centuries, with a brick vaulted undercroft, is the only surviving clue to the trading importance of this beautiful part of the coast. The Guildhall is in a small alley leading from the Quay. It is owned by English Heritage and is open all year.

This being smuggling country for centuries, there are many tales of underground tunnels leading, some say, from the Guildhall to the Friary and Wiverton Hall. There has been a grand house on this site since 1280.

It was in 1912 that Charles Rothschild bought Blakeney Point and immediately handed it over to the National Trust; thus it became the first nature reserve in Norfolk. In summer, seal trips are run at high tide. Recently a breeding colony of grey seals has become established at the end of the point in winter.

The Environment Agency has, in the last twenty years, undertaken a realignment of the

Opposite: Purple sea lavender.

THE PEDDARS WAY AND NORFOLK COAST PATH

The path at Morston.

River Glaven. The great storms of 1993 and 1996 shifted vast amounts of shingle resulting in widespread flooding of the Blakeney Freshes Special Protection Area and the village of Cley. Now the reedbeds and lagoons are home to wintering and migrating wildfowl and waders, as well as bittern, marsh harrier and the bearded tit.

For more information on this wonder of natural and man-made cooperation, visit Norfolk Wildlife Trust's Cley Marsh visitor centre in the village. It is quite fascinating. Also see:

www.norfolkwildlifetrust.org.uk

Parking around here can be difficult but the following have some access: Stiffkey, Morston, (some disabled spaces) and Blakeney (can become flooded).

You will see lots of boats and hear the tinkling of ship's paraphernalia. Some boats are obviously not going anywhere, having been left in the mud.

There is a National Trust visitor centre at Morston.

THE PEDDARS WAY AND NORFOLK COAST PATH

A misty evening in Morston.

Top: *Fine yachts reflected in the water on a summer's evening.*

Top left: *Sailboats on standby.*

Above: *A 'mud mosaic' in the drying Morston landscape.*

Left: *Morston pathway.*

Rustling reeds and glittering water in a creek at Blakeney.

Taking the floodbank as ever, head towards Blakeney. At Blakeney, enjoy the Quay – a perfect stop to have a picnic or just a breather.

Blakeney has a literary connection in that Jack Higgins did the research for the best selling 1975 novel, *The Eagle Has Landed*, while staying at the Blakeney Hotel. The subsequent film

STIFFKEY TO CLEY

There are many opportunities to 'mess about in boats' in the safety of the harbour. It is also possible to charter a barge for trips to Scolt Head Island and Holkham Bay. In the winter there is at least one Blakeney Point Seal Pup Guided Tour.

The signpost for the Path in Blakeney.

There are several fine pubs, restaurants and cafés in which to take a rest and maybe sample some famous local food and ales.

105

starred Michael Caine and Donald Pleasance. The tale concerns a group of German paratroopers who land in Norfolk during the Second World War and attempt to assassinate Churchill in his well-documented trip to the coast to check on defences.

> *'I with seven others went*
> *Our fellow man to save*
> *A heavy wave upset our boat*
> *We met a watery grave.'*
> Epitaph of John Easter, Blakeney.

Opposite: *Some boats are obviously not going anywhere and have themselves become local landmarks.*

Below: *Blakeney is a mix of mud banks, marshes and creeks with boats of every type taking advantage of the shelter offered by the twisting channels of water.*

Continue along the path and approach Cley-next-the-Sea.

There are public toilets at Morston Quay and Blakeney Quay (both disabled). It is easy to find places to eat and drink.

STIFFKEY TO CLEY

Cley-next the-Sea

A149

Salthouse

Weybourne

Coast Path

108

Chapter 10
CLEY TO WEYBOURNE

Distance: 5.2 miles

'...this corner of England which once it holds your heart is more lovely than any place on earth. Beautiful with a hint of secrecy which haunts it, as the memory of a dark and tender sadness clouds the brilliance of a summer day.'

Lilias Rider Haggard.

Section snapshot: There is lots of shingle on this part of the walk which can be hard on the legs. But what views! The vast ocean, cold and pristine, will cover you with salty spray. The sea rustles and lightly draws its breath again as it retreats. Birds whirl and whoop.

There is parking at Cley-next-the-Sea: pay and display at the beach (disabled); and Salthouse – Weybourne beach car park: pay and display (disabled).

Leaving the village on the route to Cley.

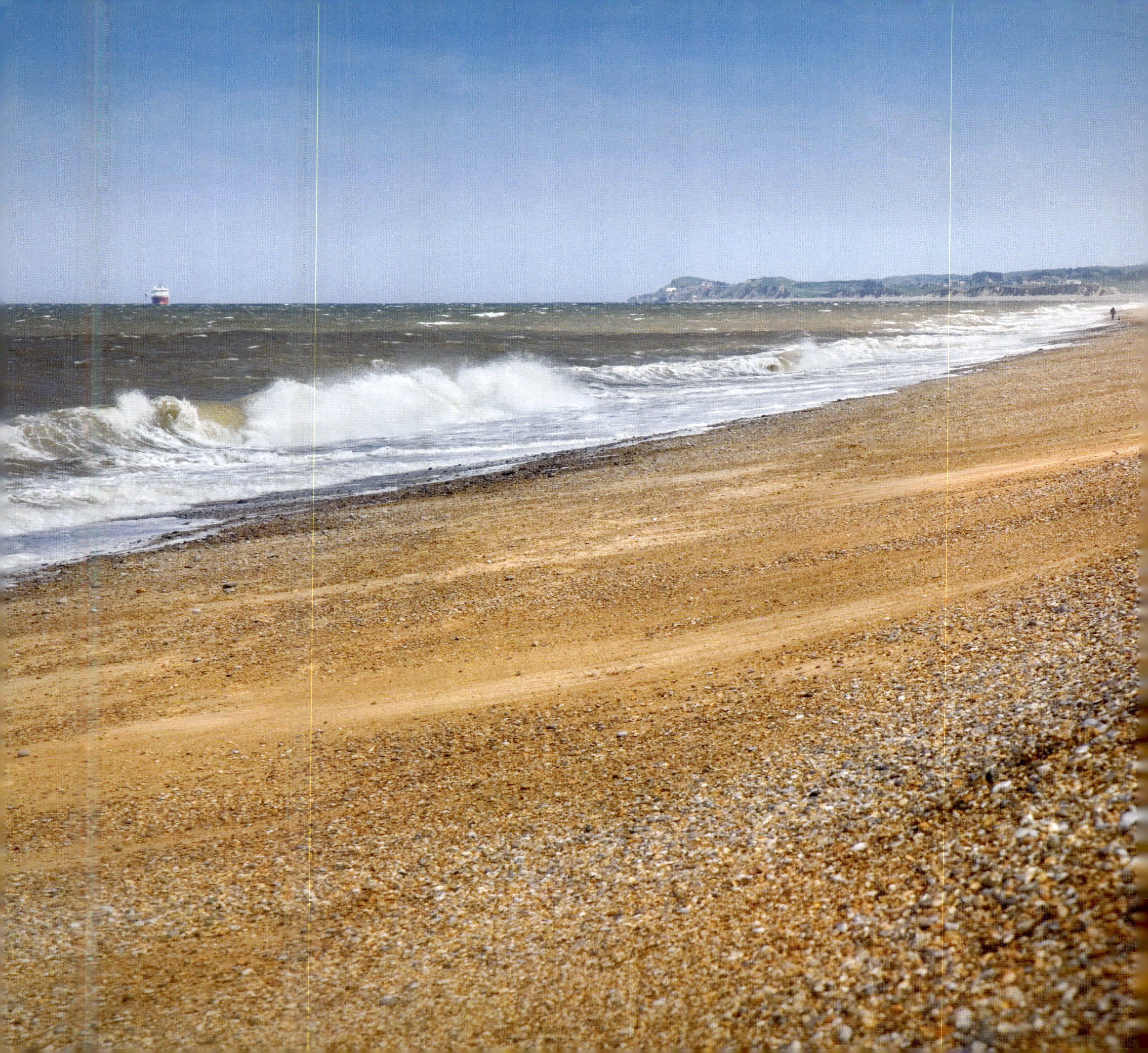

CLEY TO WEYBOURNE

The beach at Cley-next-the-sea

Cley village centre.

View towards the famous Cley windmill.

At home on Salthouse marshes.

Salthouse

Following the realignment of the River Glaven the beach and bank here have changed dramatically. The elements have taken over.

During the First and Second World Wars, the threat of German invasion on this part of the coast was very real and many reminders of this fear exist today along this section: pillboxes, gun emplacements, and stone/scaffolding obstructions on the beach.

Look out for a very rare Alan Williams cast iron turret which stands on the edge of a hill at Salthouse, and dates to about 1940.

Salthouse comes from the Old Norse and English for 'house for storing salt'. Salt was once a very precious commodity and Salthouse lies on the salt marshes in an Area of Outstanding Natural Beauty. Seven hundred years ago there were more salt pans here than anywhere in Britain. The salt would be extracted by boiling and then packed into blocks for storing. Only the nobility or wealthy merchants would have been able to afford such a rare commodity.

Sir Christopher Myngs was a famous resident, born in 1625. He was a valiant seaman who lost his life in a battle against the Dutch in 1666. He was so beloved of his men that they begged the King for a fireship in order to avenge his death (this is recorded by Pepys in his famous diaries but we are not told if the request was granted or not).

Another somewhat eccentric resident was one Onesiphorous – it means roughly 'making money' which he most certainly did – Randall. He built his house – or rather, castle, on sand and placed a cannon in front to keep away prying eyes. Often beach walkers would see a carriage carrying a beautiful lady whisking towards his domain late at night. By the time of his death in 1873, the castle had become known as 'The Folly'. It managed to survive until 1953 when it was carried away by a ferocious sea storm.

The Salthouse Sculpture Trail circular walk and Norfolk Poppy Line

If you would like to stay here for a while – and it is fantastically beautiful – you could arrange to take the Salthouse Sculpture Trail for 10 miles around the village. It takes in birdwatching, wildlife, woodland and pubs. The greater spotted woodpecker and exquisite dragonflies may be seen. As a special treat, you can take part of the trail – Holt to Kelling Heath Holt – on the North Norfolk Poppy Line: *www.nrailway.co.uk*

www.salthousehistory.co.uk is a well used and popular source of further information about the area.

The Muckleborough Collection is just off the route here and is the UK's largest privately owned military museum. Based on the former site of Weybourne Camp, used for gunnery practice until 1960, it opened its doors in 1988. Michael (now Sir Michael) Savory assembled an impressive array of military vehicles, guns and weapons along with a collection of 2500 military uniforms. It is now undergoing a complete revamp with lecture theatres and a restaurant. It really brings home the seat-of-your-trousers way that the last World War was won. Churchill came here to view the latest anti-aircraft wonders of the day and was almost killed when a projectile, although shot down successfully, landed within a whisker of his cigar. He was not pleased – the top brass were instantly sacked. www.muckleburgh.co.uk

Weybourne has evidence of population since palaeolthic times, proof of which has been unearthed in the cliffs. There are also signs of Roman activity in the area along with various finds from the Saxon period.

The church in the village grew out of a thirteenth century priory of Augustinian canons.

If you like fresh local seafood, you will be spoilt for choice in Salthouse and Weybourne. More details at www.weybourne.net

Fishing at Salthouse.

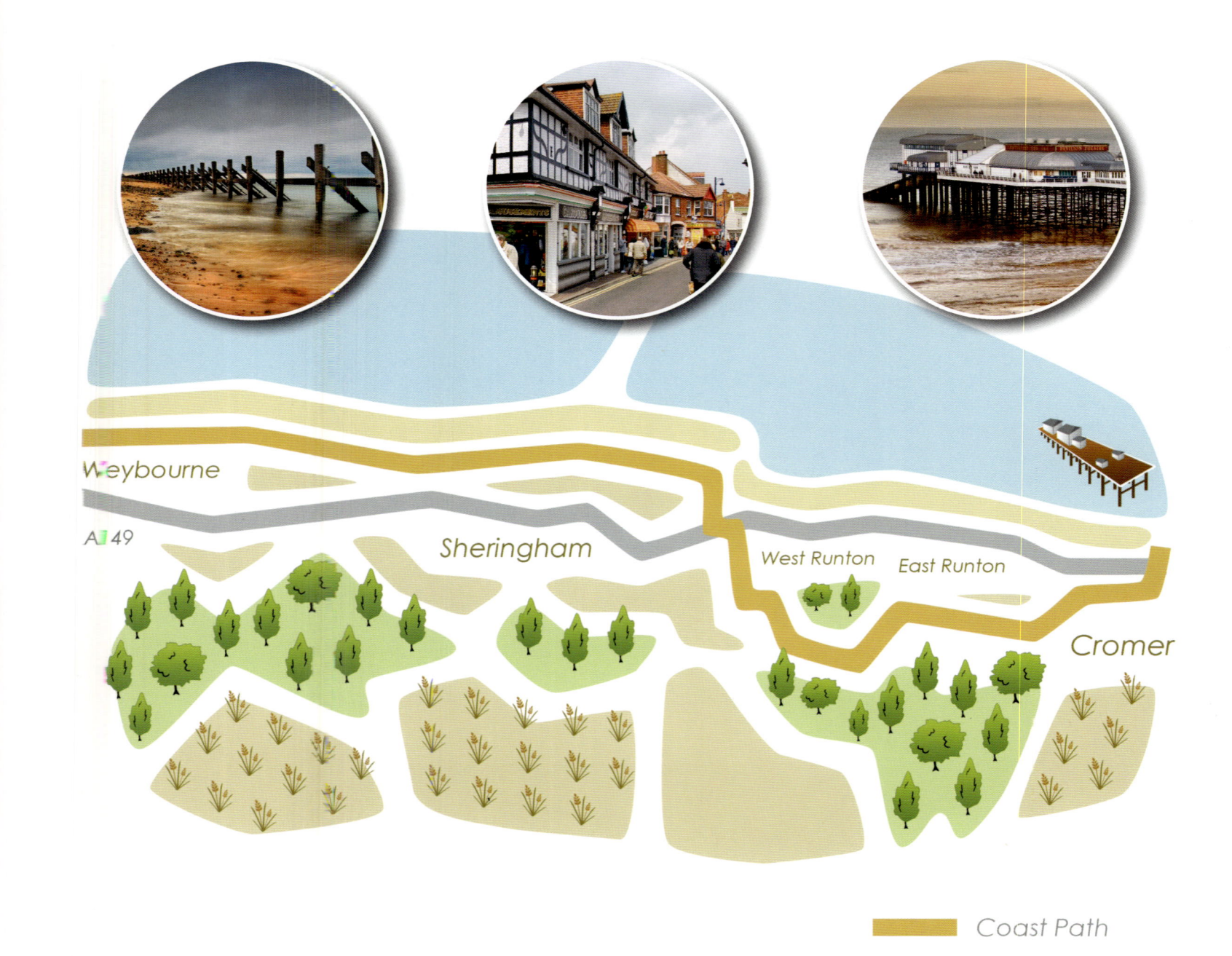

Weybourne

A149

Sheringham

West Runton   East Runton

Cromer

Coast Path

114

Chapter 11
WEYBOURNE TO CROMER

Distance: 8.6 miles

'He who would all England win, should at Weybourne Hope begin.'
Old English saying.

Section snapshot: A satisfying walk with lots of opportunities to take a break in, maybe, Sheringham or the Runtons. Experience cliff tops, woodland and seaside resorts all in one stretch. There are wonderful views looking down onto Sheringham from Beeston Bump.

Two early morning walkers at Weybourne.

Weybourne possibly means 'felon's stream' which was most likely a stretch of water in which convicted criminals were drowned, many Norfolk villages having something similar. There has certainly never been a shortage of villains as smuggling vast quantities of gin, tobacco and brandy was very much the backbone of the 'economy' in days gone by. If you lived by the sea and were prepared to turn a blind eye to goings-on in the night, you could find a 'present' on your doorstep in the morning.

Weybourne has very deep water offshore and, from the time of the Spanish Armada in 1588 right up to the Second World War, has consequently been seen as England's most vulnerable spot for hostile troop landings. In the Second World War an exclusion zone was established which extended 10 miles out into the sea.

The station is just outside the village centre and is on the 'Poppy Line' running from Sheringham to Holt and will take you on an unforgettable ten mile trip among the most glorious Norfolk country.

Dad's Army used the local station as the setting for the episode 'The Royal Train.'

On the path to Weybourne.

Weybourne beach.

THE PEDDARS WAY AND NORFOLK COAST PATH

This very beautiful, peaceful place is an ideal stopping off point just to walk the cliffs, fish – it is very popular with anglers – or take a excursion to nearby Sheringham Park, only rivalled by Sandringham for wonderful rhododendrons in hues of magenta, white, lavender and yellow.

Weybourne beach car park is pay and display (disabled).

From Weybourne beach car park take the cliff top towards Sheringham. Follow the path through two kissing gates, past the lifeboat cottage, and continue along the cliff top.

Views of the Path from Weybourne to Sheringham.

THE PEDDARS WAY AND NORFOLK COAST PATH

Perfect jogging country between Weybourne and Sheringham.

Sheringham

A petition of 1673 related that the people of Sheringham were *'afraid every night ye enemy should come ashore and fire our towne when we be in our beds; for ye houses stand very close together and all ye houses thatched with straw, that in one hours time ye towne may be burnt, for we have nothing to resist them but one gun with a broken carriage and foure musquetts which we bought at our own cost and charges.'* (From *East Anglia* by Hugh Meredith).

When you have passed the National Trust's Sheringham Park, keep walking the cliff edge past the golf course. The cliffs are flaky here, falling in some parts and it is essential to keep well back from the edge. You will soon head downward to Sheringham.

Sheringham has a strong – usually harmonious but not always – rivalry with nearby Cromer, each claiming to be the North Norfolk coast's premier resort. In particular, you must

Jogging on Sheringham beach.

Marvellous views to Sheringham from Beeston Bump.

Above: *Sheringham beach is popular with families.*

Top: *The local ice cream is not to be missed!*

Sheringham town centre offers a diverse range of shops, pubs and cafés.

Sheringham Gardens.

be either a Sheringham or a Cromer man: you must choose. Sheringham proclaims itself to be 'The Jewel of the Norfolk Coast'. Loudly extolling the virtues of the rival town in a pub or café is not recommended.

Once, there was both an upper and a lower Sheringham but today the town is centred around the High Street with an unusual and interesting collection of shops – including dealers in art and crafts, fishing tackle, antiques and cafés. If you have not yet tried North Norfolk's crabs, lobsters and whelks, this is an excellent time – there are innumerable spots to picnic overlooking the immense ocean.

The Sheringham lifeboat is justly renowned for saving hundreds of lives. Interestingly, it needs to be launched by a tractor pulling it into the sea as there is no suitable raised harbour. The original RNLI lifeboat station has been refurbished in recent years and acts as a general purpose meeting house. The local museum, called the Mo, includes a collection of old lifeboats.

THE PEDDARS WAY AND NORFOLK COAST PATH

A panoramic view of Sheringham.

*'Up comrades, gather to the boat, the rocket line prepare
For many a gallant man tonight is battling with despair
The squall comes roaring onward, driving right across the sea,
And who's the craven that shall say "no call there for me".*

*So may the God of heaven e'en now their earnest efforts bless,
May He who prospereth our way now give them good success.'*

Extract from a poem by Miss Anna Gurney of Sheringham
on the launching of the lifeboat *Augusta* in 1838.

The railway connection with Norwich survives and is known as the Bittern Line.

Do try to visit St Joseph Roman Catholic church, a rare building of its type by Sir Giles Gilbert Scott. It took six years to build, being consecrated in 1908. Some think it resembles a modern factory from the outside.

Famous residents include the poet, Stephen Spender (1909-1995) and, on a lighter note, Allan Smethurst, the 'singing postman' (1927-2000). Sheringham also boasts His Royal Highness King Nicholas I, previously known as Nick Copeman, who set up his kingdom from a caravan just outside the town.

Walk past the boating pond, and descend the slopes to the promenade, past the old lifeboat house and walk along the upper prom. Climb onto Beeston Bump. During the last war, a secret listening station was set up on the Bump in order to track enemy ships. There is no sign of it now as it was made of wood and dismantled at the end of the conflict. Follow the trail again from here towards West Runton.

THE PEDDARS WAY AND NORFOLK COAST PATH

Sheringham to West Runton.

Daniel, photographer for this book, takes up the story here as he has very vivid memories of family holidays at West Runton. The following extract is taken from *Norfolk: Exploring the Land of Wide Skies* (Halsgrove) by the present authors.

'The Runtons, East and West, are quaint villages and became a family favourite throughout the summer months. Sandy in a few places, regular visitors will notice an occasional change in the way the shoreline appears, thanks to where the tide decides to position the numerous collections of stones and seaweed patches, which will sometimes lead to a slightly further walk to find that perfect bump-free spot for your picnic basket.

A common scenario which makes me smile is watching families pack on to the hard sands that appear when the tide is out, to then have to dash back to the drier stonier sands when the inevitable happens. West Runton regulars will have sourced the best sandy positions safe from the tide earlier in the day.

West Runton has been our family holiday destination for many years, always timing it to coincide with the Cromer Carnival week in August. I recall great numbers of the family creating a huge arc of windbreaks. It was indeed behind the windbreaks that I used to get up to great

View from the cliffs at West Runton.

There are several places to break your stay at West Runton including the well-known Links Hotel.

Looking towards West Runton and Beeston Bump.

mischief. I remember quietly positioning myself behind my poor Dad and attempting to dig under the windbreak and his deck chair in the hope of a sudden tip backwards! Another fun game was digging a hole where somebody had been sitting on their towel, placing the towel back over the top and waiting for my next victim. Now I'm a little older I look back and realise how much of a tease I was! (But it was fun all the same).

During the low tide, the sea will slowly reveal a hidden landscape that starts with exposure of a few rock pools and extends into crabbing heaven for some – brave beginners beware of sharp pincers! On an exceptionally low scouring tide you are treated to an ancient foreshore of chalk, clay and rock formations. On closer inspection you will find an abundance of sea creatures, both live and fossilised dating back to Jurassic and Cretaceous periods – Belemites are a common find (these are shaped like a bullet).

Fossils can also be found in exposed areas of the cliff known as the Cromer Forest Bed (which dates back 500,000-700,000 years). Indeed, it was the discovery of a very special find in the early 1990s that put West Runton on the geological map. After a particularly stormy winter night, fossilised remains of a large pelvic bone were discovered. Over the next few years as more bones were uncovered it became clear that a major find may be on the cards. An excavation soon revealed the largest and most complete elephant skeleton to date. This is now famously known as the "West Runton Elephant" and some of the bones can be seen on display at Cromer Museum. West Runton Beach café has some photos from the excavation.

If you love horses then don't miss the Shire Horse Centre with Shire-Horse pulled rides or take a guided trek around the local countryside'.

Sea defences, West Runton.

Low tide at West Runton.

At Beeston Bump (left) the Path comes inland for a short while before once more heading for the coast. This is the view from Calves Well Lane, West Runton towards the sea.

Cromer

*'Pray God lead us,
Pray God speed us;
From all evil defend us;
Fish for our pains God send us.
Well to fish and well to haul,
And what he pleases to pay all.
A fine night to land our nets,
And safe in with the land.
Pray God hear my prayer.'*
Ancient Cromer fisherman's prayer.

Cromer fisherman used to be famous for two things primarily – great boldness in the face of real danger, and an almost childish terror of the supernatural. We talk about the most famous myth – or not at all, say many – the Black Shuk, in a moment, as well as some other supernatural beliefs.

Cromer pier as dawn breaks.

Cromer pier under the primrose skies
so beloved of Norfolk writers.

THE PEDDARS WAY AND NORFOLK COAST PATH

A fine specimen of the incomparable Cromer crab.

Cromer crabs are said to be supreme and this is because the ground on which they feed is rich in food. Shawn is the latest generation of a fishing family – he first went out when he was seven and was 'sick as a dog' – and takes out his boat, with his mate, Paul, at four in the morning. They fish for about three hours and then it is home for breakfast. Some fishermen fish all year but the season really starts in March. 'The traditional saying is that crabbing goes on until Wimbledon,' Shawn says. 'Then lobsters replace crabs for about six weeks and then it's back to crabs again.' Once upon a time herrings reigned supreme along the coast but, alas, no longer. This is partly because they are no longer so plentiful but also, according to Shawn, that the modern cook finds them too fiddly to prepare.

Shawn.

The famous Cromer lifeboat

Shawn also served for some years on the lifeboat. Many fishermen do. One of the most illustrious sons of Cromer is Coxswain Henry George Blogg who saved lives for an incredible fifty-three years. In that time he rescued 873 people and was awarded the George Cross and the British Empire Medal.

Cromer cliffs

The Cromer Forest Bed formation is exposed at intervals along the Norfolk coast from Weybourne to Kessingland. The ancient forest bed was formed some 780-450,000 years ago. As the bed in the form of cliffs continues to be eroded there are a wealth of fossils to be found.

> '...the best of all the sea-bathing places. A fine open sea...and very pure air...'
> Jane Austen in *Emma* published 1816.

There used to be another settlement, called Shipden, but which is now lost to the sea: '*Due north, and twenty one miles as the crow flies from the Castle Hill of Norwich, stands huddled into a*

Cromer Gardens – one of thousands of spots to have your picnic in and around the town.

THE PEDDARS WAY AND NORFOLK COAST PATH

hollow and along the cliff edge, the little village of Cromer, and a quarter of a mile out to sea the tide rolls in and rolls out over the lost town of Shipden.

Once or twice in the year, at the very dregs of the lowest neap tides, the water recedes beyond broken foundations matted with seaweed – long ridges of what were once great walls, but which now hardly peep above the sand, and a great overturned mass of squared flint work, which the fishermen call the "Church Rock", once the tower of Shipden Church.' (From *East Anglia* by Hugh Meredith.)

Angry stormclouds gather over Cromer cliffs.

Poppyland

Today, the area around Sheringham and Cromer attracts thousands of visitors each summer to see the golden sands, behind which poppies rise up in a glorious ark of scarlet. Add the green of the trees to the huge metallic blue skies and the effect is quite beyond beautiful.

It was, in fact, a journalist from the *Daily Telegraph* called Clement Scott who coined the term 'Poppyland'. He had been sent by his paper to find out why this area had suddenly become *the* place to come for sea air and holidays. He immediately fell in love with the coast and also a local miller's daughter, Louie Jermy. Scott was responsible for many other famous artists coming down, some of whom built beautiful houses – Oscar Wilde, A.C. Swinburne and Alfred, Lord Tennyson were all smitten. For a number of years, Sidestrand, where Scott lived, must have been the richest small settlement in the land.

The term 'Poppyland' first appears in a poem called 'The Garden of Sleep' that Scott wrote in the graveyard of Sidestrand church – just a couple of easy miles from Cromer, the end of this particular trail. This is where his love, Louie, is buried. The final verse reads:

The North Norfolk Railway, known affectionately as the Poppy Line, runs from Sheringham to Holt taking in some of the finest scenery.

*'In my garden of sleep, where red poppies are spread,
I wait for the living, alone with the dead!
For a tower in ruins stands guard o'er the deep,
At whose feet are green graves of dear women asleep!
Did they love as I love, when they lived by the sea?
Did they wait as I wait, for the days that may be?
Was it hope or fulfilling that entered each breast,
Ere death gave release, and the poppies gave rest?
O! Life of my life! On the cliffs by the sea,
By graves in the grass, I am waiting for thee!
Sleep! Sleep!
In the Dews of the Deep!
Sleep, my Poppy-land,
Sleep!'*

.. for a tower in ruins stands guard o'er the deep...' (reproduced with permission, Picture Norfolk Library).

**'The sea against the cliffs doth daily beat,
And ever tide into the land doth eat.'**
John Taylor, poet (1580-1653).

Sherlock Holmes and Cromer

Cromer is famous in literary terms as the town from which Arthur Conan Doyle gained the idea for one of the best-loved Sherlock Holmes stories, *The Hound of the Baskervilles*. In 1901 he had returned from South Africa where he had been collecting data for the UK government on the state of the Army which led in turn to a damning but practical report on how best to raise health and morale in British Armed forces world-wide. It was this which led to his knighthood (although many people understandably think it must have been his literary work). He was, unfortunately, stricken badly with enteric fever and he came to Cromer to recuperate. Whilst here, he learnt the story of the Black Shuk which locals believed prowled along this coastline and would tear the throat out of anyone unlucky enough to cross its path. Transferring the story to the chilling loneliness of Dartmoor, one of the great iconic tales of the age was born: *The Hound of the Baskervilles* was released the following year and was an immediate world-wide sensation.

There is another twist in this tale in that a journalist called Bertram Fletcher Robinson, who accompanied Doyle on his trip, is claimed by many to have been the originator of the idea for the tale and should, they say, have been credited with co-authorship of the story. Doyle would have none of it, however, and Robinson died not long after at the young age of 37. The argument continues – several excellent novels have been written based on these events – right up to the present.

> *'And a dreadful thing from the cliff did spring,*
> *And its wild bark thrill'd around,*
> *His eyes had the glow of the fires below,*
> *'Twas the form of the Spectre Hound.'*
>
> Anonymous.

Yet a further variation claims that *The Hound of the Baskervilles* is based on the family history of the Cabbell family. The story goes that Conan Doyle and Robinson were invited to dinner at Cromer Hall (just outside the town) by Benjamin Bond Cabbell and told how his ancestor, Richard, Lord of Brook Manor and Buckfastleigh, had been the victim of a devil dog. The Lord had heard of his wife's unfaithfulness and she fled onto Dartmoor. He followed and stabbed her to death but was then killed by a gigantic hound: he was found the following morning with his throat torn out.

It is easy to be sceptical as to claims about the Black Shuk. Even today, some locals fervently believe in the creature. As we say above, superstition has always had large sway in this area of the world. There are those who say, also, that the dog – although indeed existing – is nonetheless a gentle soul who has been morosely searching for his shipwrecked master since 1709.

There is a chilling story told in a book (*People and Places in Marshland*, Cecil Palmer, London) by Christophe Marlowe who was undertaking a bicycle tour of the area in 1927. Christopher had been relaxing in a pub and expressed the view that the Black Shuk was just a means of gaining tourist revenue. The locals were appalled that he doubted the existence of the creature. So he made a bet – he would spend the night just off the beach and prove they were wrong. Briefly told, he arranged to take a room in a lonely cottage a few hundred yards from where the 'Shuk' was reputed to roam. Despite the empassioned pleas of his host not to venture out after dark, he did just that. Briefly put, he saw the creature as it sniffed along the coast and prepared to find him in his hideaway. Then:

'With a yell of terror I jumped up from the hollow and fled. Not once did I look behind, but I felt that the creature was in pursuit. Never have I run as I ran that night. Stumbling, cursing, breathing heavily, I tore up the lane and at last gained the threshold of the cottage…

… as the bolt was undone and the key turned I glanced around to see a pair of ferocious eyes fixed upon me and to feel on my neck a scorching breath. The hound was about to spring as the door opened and I fell fainting into the arms of my host.'

The lantern men also are believed to operate along the coast. These are wispy vapours that rise from the ground and chase you. If they catch you they, worse that the Death Eaters in the Harry Potter books, will suck all life from you (the Death Eaters 'merely' extract all joy). If you see them, the thing to do is to throw yourself on the ground whilst holding your breath for as long as possible. Hopefully, they will pass by looking another victim.

During a storm, some believe that you can hear the cries of drowned sailors who are calling on the crews of any ships in the area to join them at the bottom of the ocean.

> 'A little way out to sea there is a spot, they say, just opposite a particular cliff, where the captain of some old ship was drowned, and there more than once fishermen have heard sounds like a human voice coming up from the water; whichever way they pull, the voice is in the other direction, 'til at last, on a sudden, it changes, and comes just beneath their boat like the last wild cry of a man sinking hopelessly. Then if they are wise they settle down to their oars, and row for life to shore; for life it is – for they are lucky if they reach home in time to escape the squall which is sure to follow.'
> Article in local publication about 1860.

The inventor of the bagless vacuum cleaner and much more, Sir James Dyson, was born in Cromer and went to school in Holt.

Famous author and writer, Stephen Fry recounts in his autobiography *Moab Is My Washpot* how he walked 'two hundred miles' along the corridors of the Hotel de Paris while working as a waiter here.

> 'There was an old person from Cromer
> Who stood on one leg to read Homer;
> When he found he grew stiff, he jumped over the cliff
> Which concluded that Person from Cromer.'
> Edward Lear (1812 – 1888).

There are many different walks you can take at Cromer if you have any energy left by this time. A gentle stroll on the pier in relaxing. Many holidaymakers like to stroll a couple of miles further, along the beach to Overstrand, taking in the cliffs and exploring the rockpools.

Chapter 12
PRACTICAL THINGS

'First, have a definite, clear practical ideal; a goal, an objective. Second, have the necessary means to achieve your ends; wisdom, money, materials, and methods.'

Aristotle (384 -322 BC).

Accommodation. Accommodation is available throughout the Peddars Way and North Norfolk Coast Path, although limited in some parts. If you plan to book into a guest house, B and B or hotel, make sure you book before beginning the walk. You can also camp as well as using Youth Hostels in some places (despite their name, they are for people of all ages and fantastic value for money). We have not provided specific details and prices in this book as the situation is continually changing. However, the internet is excellent for research as well as local information centres and either of these sources will give you the very latest and accurate information on places to stay during your walk.

Baggage carriers. Sometimes you can hire the services of baggage carriers who will collect your luggage just after breakfast and deliver it to your evening location. Taxis also sometimes provide this service. Best to contact a tourist information centre along the route, probably in a large town like Hunstanton or Cromer for up-to-date details.

Cycling. Pretty much all of the Peddars Way can be explored by bike, although there are a few sections where cyclists must take an alternative route. Be careful of very sharp flints, especially in the Brecks area and always have your tyre puncture repair kit handy. Cycling is NOT allowed on the Norfolk Coast Path but there is an alternative and specially created cycleway, just a little inland. A map of this is available from tourist information centres for a few pounds.

Disabled access. One of the great joys of the route is that large sections are perfectly accessible to disabled people. The Peddars Way is generally flat. As for the spectacular Norfolk Coast, a good centre for exploration is either Sheringham or Cromer as seaside parking is easy. Snettisham Bird Reserve has special facilities for wheelchairs.

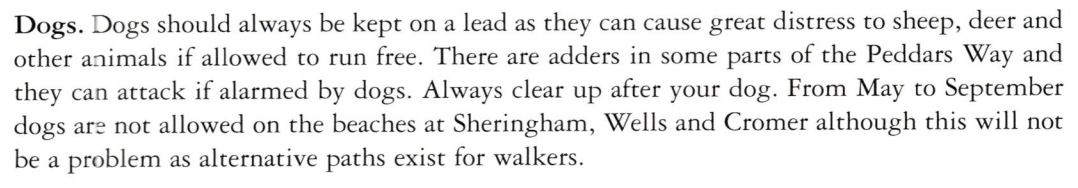

Dogs. Dogs should always be kept on a lead as they can cause great distress to sheep, deer and other animals if allowed to run free. There are adders in some parts of the Peddars Way and they can attack if alarmed by dogs. Always clear up after your dog. From May to September dogs are not allowed on the beaches at Sheringham, Wells and Cromer although this will not be a problem as alternative paths exist for walkers.

Essentials to take along. It is really important to be as light as possible so be ruthless – will you really read that book on the trip? If you are going with a.n.other, do you need two cameras? Surely a week's supply of fruit isn't necessary as you can buy as you go?

A big **rucksack** is about 75 litres and a small one, maybe 30. If you are going camping, the big one is necessary (for the tent, poles and so on), but if you have booked accommodation in a hostel or B and B in advance, it most certainly is not.

These are some things you WILL need:

A detailed map of the route.

Money – calculate how much you may spend in a day and, if it is not too much, take cash. If you are worried about having so much on you, carry a debit card.

Boots – strong, broken in and comfortable. Several pairs of **socks**, preferably made of natural fibres. **Flip flops** for that 'ah!' moment in the evening when the boots come off. **For the body** – cotton underlayer; outer layer to keep you warm – maybe a fleece jacket; a waterproof outer garment to keep you dry. **For the legs** – something very comfortable and quick drying like track suit bottoms and, if you have room, a pair of shorts. **Underwear** – several changes of underwear. **For the extremities** – warm hat and gloves. **Toiletries** – whatever you use at home (if not going alone, can you share some items?). Plus **sun lotion** – absolutely essential. A **small first aid kit** (you can buy very cleverly compacted ones from high street chemists).

Don't forget at least a litre bottle of **water** per person, maybe even two if you are feeling strong. Sometimes you can feel tired but not thirsty but what is really happening is that your body is dehydrated. Plus **tissues** and a **torch**.

GPS. GPS technology can be a useful supplement to a map but never a replacement for it. It can quickly establish your whereabouts if you are unsure but, of course, once the power is run-down it is useless.

Horses. Much of the Peddars Way can be experienced on horseback, although riders should be prepared to take an alternative route sometimes. You CANNOT ride on the Norfolk Coast Path.

How difficult? Neither part of the route is particularly challenging, although shingle and sand on the Norfolk Coast can be hard on the legs, especially after a day's walking. There are dangers, too, such as the saltmarshes, cliff-top walks and, down below, the ever-present possibility of getting trapped by the tide. On the Peddars Way section, distances can be deceptive – always remember to take a good supply of water; wear a hat and be generous with the suntan lotion. On the whole, though, with care and planning, the whole of the route is fine for reasonably able-bodied people of all ages.

How long? The whole route is about 96 miles. Experienced and super-fit folk can finish it in about three days. Most, however, take maybe eight or nine days. In preparing this book, we have had great enjoyment in veering slightly 'off course' now and again and, if you do this, the walk can take almost as long as you like. There is so much of interest just beyond the tree you can see in the mist at the edge of the next field…

Local Food. Much has changed about Norfolk's reputation for fine food in recent years. It used to be famous for mustard – Colman's of course – turkeys, sugarbeet, kippers, Cromer crabs and not much else. Nowadays you can experience fabulous Norfolk cakes, beef, cider, beer, wines, cheeses, breads, organic vegetables, honey, preserves, pickles, pork pies, sausages and home-smoked treats. In many inns and pubs along the route – especially along the coast – you will also be able to take relatively inexpensive lunches and dinners cooked by the best chefs in the land and washed down by beers of supreme quality and distinctiveness. The authors of this book recently had the great good fortune to set out all over the county to research – and taste! – Norfolk foods of every type. The results are published in our *Norfolk Food Heroes* (Halsgrove) available from bookshops county-wide and Amazon.

Medical. The worst that will happen to most walkers is the occasional blister. Make sure your boots are thoroughly 'worn in' before walking any distance and keep them dry inside. If you get a blister treat it with some zinc oxide tape and cover with a dry sterile dressing. The strong winds and icy rain of Norfolk also makes the threat of hypothermia a real one if you are not wearing adequate clothing and not eating and drinking properly. If you feel cold and shivery, take shelter and warmth as soon as possible and drink something warm. Hyperthermia can also be extremely unpleasant and, in extreme cases, fatal. This is caused by dehydration: hence our comments about always carrying at least a litre of fluid with you and topping up whenever possible. Heat stroke is also possible and, if you feel fatigue, giddy, bad-tempered or just 'odd', take shelter in the shade. Cold wet towelling-down of the sufferer should help. Sunburn can be avoided by liberally applying a good sun screen to all parts of exposed skin on your face and body and wearing a hat.

As a general rule, always seek medical assistance at the first available opportunity if in any doubt at all as to what the problem may be.

Medical benefits of walking have been proved by a year-long trial carried out by the University of Pittsburgh in the USA and reported by the BBC in 2011. The trial showed that walking for forty minutes a few times a week could preserve memory and keep brains sharper. It also found that it is never too late to begin a walking routine and any amount, however modest, will help protect the brain from decline.

Minimum impact walking. This is a trendy mantra these days and is not, as might at first appear, to do with bumping into as few things as possible (although this is a good idea). It is really all about respect for the countryside and common sense. Don't drop litter. Don't light fires. Close all gates after you. Keep the dog under control. Ask permission before setting up camp. Leave flowers for others to enjoy. Clean up after your pet. Check the tide tables before venturing onto the beach (these can be obtained from information centres).

Weather. The climate in East Anglia is to some degree continental, with the area you will walk subject to less rain than other parts of the UK. It is at the centre of four air masses, northerlies, southerlies, easterlies and westerlies which can bring, respectively, icy, warm, windy and wet conditions in almost any variation. There is really nowhere else in the UK where weather will play such a large and unpredictable part in your adventures! Check out the situation at www.bbc.co.uk/weather

When to go? Absolutely any time of the year is fine and each has a special charm. Winter can be great – crisp, clear and cold; spring sees new life and flora; summer is very busy and you will often get to chat with fellow walkers; and autumn is spectacular with summer-migrating birds leaving and making way for new arrivals from Scandinavia and eastern Europe. Beware the Norfolk weather, though, as storms and winds can sweep you off your feet in an instant!

Which way? This book takes you from the quieter Peddars Way to the spectacular coast. Most people choose this but you will always meet some coming the opposite way, and a chat on the best route/upcoming hazards/places to eat etc. can be very useful.

Appendix 1
A guide to some of the place names encountered along the Peddars Way and Norfolk Coast Path

In the main text, we give some meanings of the place names you may encounter on the trail. Here are a few more. Sometimes, it has to be said, we just do not know as the language has changed so much in the last 1000 years, and so some are simply our best guess…

Beeston – place (ton) where trade takes place or of rushes
Binham – Bynna's homestead
Blackwater Carr – dark water (Blackwater) rock (Carr)
Blakeney – possibly black island
Brancaster – camp (caster) of broom
Brandon – hill (don) of broom
Buckenham Tofts – Toft probably site of a dwelling
Buckenham – probably a name, Bucca's homestead
Burnham – homestead by a stream
Burnham Deepdale – possibly homestead by deep water
Burnham Staithe – Staithe probably landing place on a river
Castle Acre – Acre probably plot of land
Castle Rising – perhaps Castle of Risa'a folk
Cley – area of clay soil
Cromer – pond (mere) where crows gather
Elveden – valley (den) of swans
Great Bircham – larger (Great) site (ham) of newly cultivated land (Old English Bricha)
Heacham – homestead (ham) with a sluice (hec)
Holkham – homestead (ham) in a hollow
Houghton – enclosure on a hill projectory
Holme – small island
Hunstanton – enclosure belonging to Hunstan
Kessingland – the place of Cyssi's folk
Langford – possibly Landa's ford
Little Cressingham – smaller (Little) homestead (ham) of the people from Cresswell

Lynford – possibly ford on the road to Lynn (Kings Lynn)
Massingham – homestead (ham) of Maessa's people
Mildenhall – probably the nook (hall) of the mild one (Milda), or Milden may be a name
Morston – enclosure (ton) on the marsh
Pickenham – homestead of Pica
Runton – farm of Runa or Runi
Salthouse – literally house for storing salt
Sandringham – homestead (ham) of the sandy ones
Sedgeford – possibly ford where sedge grows; alternatively it may mean stream that trickles
Sheringham – homestead (ham) of Scira's people
Shipden – valley (den) of the sheep
Snettisham – homestead (ham) of Snettis
Stanford – ford with many stones (stan is Old English for stones)
Stiffkey – island of tree stumps
Sturston – enclosure (ton) of Styrr
Swaffham – homestead of the Swabian people
Thetford – ford of the people (perhaps important ford)
Thornham – homestead (ham) where thorn bushes grow
Threxton – unsure but possibly enclosure (ton) that is dirty (threx OE for dirt)
Walsingham – homestead (ham) of Wael's folk
Wells – springs
Weybourne – probably felon's stream, a place of execution by drowning for criminals

Appendix 2
Norfolk Songline verses. Each stone bears an inscription. Here are the verses you will see on the trail.

The footprint of our ancestors
Familiar as our own faces
Remote as fossils
Written on clay
And washed away
Over and Over
Over and Over

Surveyors have made their lines on the land
Trapping Albion in a net of roads
A taut web on the edge of empire

The piety of every man and every woman's whispered prayer
Clasped in the grain of wood and stone and in the grace of ancient air

From Blackwater Carr to Seagate
Since the plough first broke the bread of land
Pightles and pieces plots and pastures
To every man his stony acre

And I being here have been part of all this
Caught and thrown like sun on water
Have entered into all around me

Appendix 3
Norfolk language: a few unfamiliar words you may hear on the trail

Bittern	*Buttle*	Ladybird	*Bishy-barney-bee*
Causeway (eg across a saltmarsh)	*Carnser*	Narrow lane	*Loke*
Chat	*Mardle*	Neighbour	*Bor*
Chimney	*Chimley*	Nonsense	*Squit*
Filthy	*Muckwash*	Odd	*Rum*
Donkey	*Dickey*	Muddy	*Claggy*
Girl	*Mawther*	Small	*Titty-Totty*
Heron	*Harnser*	Snail	*Dodman*
Jackdaw	*Caddow*	Stream	*Cockey*
Meadow	*Pightle*	Stretch of sandy sealine	*Dene*